Black Belt Karate

Black Belt Karate

CHRIS THOMPSON

BLUE SNAKE BOOKS
BERKELEY, CALIFORNIA

BLUE SNAKE BOOKS
BERKELEY, CALIFORNIA

Published by Blue Snake Books
Blue Snake Books are distributed by
North Atlantic Books, P.O. Box 12327, Berkeley, California 94712

Black Belt Karate is sponsored by the Society for the Study of Native Arts and Sciences, a nonprofit educational corporation whose goals are to develop an educational and cross-cultural perspective linking various scientific, social, and artistic fields; to nurture a holistic view of arts, sciences, humanities, and healing; and to publish and distribute literature on the relationship of mind, body, and nature.

North Atlantic Books' publications are available through most bookstores. For further information, call 800-733-3000 or visit our websites at www.northatlanticbooks.com and www.bluesnakebooks.com.

PLEASE NOTE: The creators and publishers of this book disclaim any liabilities for loss in connection with following any of the practices, exercises, and advice contained herein. To reduce the chance of injury or any other harm, the reader should consult a professional before undertaking this or any other martial arts, movement, meditative arts, health, or exercise program. The instructions and advice printed in this book are not in any way intended as a substitute for medical, mental, or emotional counseling with a licensed physician or healthcare provider.

ISBN 13: 978-1-58394-254-3

CIP data available upon request.

1 2 3 4 5 6 7 8 9
14 13 12 11 10 09 08
Printed and bound in Malaysia by Times Offset (M) Sdn Bnd
Reproduction by Pica Digital Pte Ltd, Singapore

Senior Editor: Sarah Goulding
Designer: Roger Hammond
Illustrator: Stephen Dew
Photography: Mike Holdsworth
Production: Marion Storz
Publishing Director: Rosemary Wilkinson

Contents

Preface

Karate is the art of unarmed combat using parts of the body as weapons: hands, feet, elbows, knees, and even the head. It has also become an exciting sport providing a fascinating and exhilarating challenge for anyone taking it up, regardless of age or sex. Through systematic and prolonged training, mental as well as physical, over many years, many people can become proficient in the art.

There are many reasons why people are attracted to karate. It still holds an air of mystery, and to be a "black belt" is a title that appeals to many. To be able to defend yourself in any situation, without requiring weapons other than those you were born with, is inspirational. Obviously, most people who have never taken up the art of karate will have heard of its benefits, such as gaining greater fitness and confidence. Yet there is much, much more that karate has to offer. An inner peace can be developed as well as a feeling of well-being. I believe karate can make you a better person. I hope you find, or have found, a *sensei* (teacher) who will guide you the right way on your long and enjoyable road of training in karate-do.

This book is aimed at students who have already started the long path in the study of karate. The techniques shown are not for beginners in the art, but for the intermediate student and black belts—therefore, a certain

Left: The stance *gyaku nekoaschi-dachi* (reverse cat stance) where the attacker has placed 70 percent of his body weight onto the front leg to carry out a strike to the head.
Below: The attacker on the right strikes to his opponent's face with a left *yonhon nukite jodan* (four-finger spear hand at head height).

degree of skill must have been obtained before embarking on the techniques shown here.

To be capable of looking after yourself, all aspects of self-defense must be practiced regularly, not just kicking, striking, and punching. Karate-do encapsulates all of this, and the movements must be repeated as often as possible, whether you are training on your own, or with a partner. The aim of all karate practice is to make techniques instinctive, delivered without any hesitation whatsoever.

Black Belt Karate gives a brief history of how the karate we are now studying came into being, and how it has developed from the latter part of the last century, right up to the modern day. The book also describes how sport competition karate is now the driving force behind many karate schools, which makes it very attractive to younger practitioners. The lack of emphasis in many karate schools on traditional karate values and ethos has led to a fall in the number of adult students, but this book is suitable for all ages, and aims to help you further your karate education and your all-around development.

Left: A reinforced block using the right forearm. **Right:** *Migi morote uke* delivered in right back stance, *kokutsu dachi*.

Introduction to karate

Karate is an exciting and exhilarating art and is open to everybody. Size, sex, and height do not matter; you can become proficient at karate as long as you start learning from an expert *sensei* (which means "teacher"—literally, "one who has gone before"). Having a good *sensei* to guide you not only means that he or she can make you proficient and capable of looking after yourself, but also carries a lot of other benefits. These include confidence-building, improved self-discipline, physical fitness, and self-protection. With confidence, an aura is given out, hopefully making karate practitioners less of a target to a bully.

There are so many positive character-building attributes to karate. Many organizations aim to instill more humility, courtesy, and integrity in their students with regular and vigorous training. The aim for all students, as well as teachers, is to respect others who show commitment, to possess equanimity, and to be honest and responsible. The whole ethos of studying karate-do is a positive one.

Left: The opening movement from the Japanese Karate Association Shotokan *kata sochin.*
Below: Striking an opponent's leg in prearranged pairwork.

What to look for in a club

To acquire skills in karate, you must first find a good club and a good *sensei*. Even if you are not a complete beginner, you may be changing clubs, moving from one town or city to another, or even moving to another country. Some of the elements you need to consider before committing yourself to a particular club are described here.

First, go along and watch a local club in progress for the full session. See how the *sensei* teaches and how they conduct themselves. There is nothing wrong with asking the instructor questions, no matter what their dan rank or what country you are in. Ask what style is being practiced, whether the club belongs to a governing body that is world-recognized, and whether the students and club are fully insured. An instructor who took umbrage at any of these questions would give me cause for concern, and there is no reasonable basis to avoid any of these pertinent questions.

You may also wish to know the emphasis toward which the karate class is geared. Is it primarily sport

karate or is it based more on traditional aspects of self-defense?

The next element to consider is the equipment needed to start karate training. Find out if the club will provide a *gi* (karate suit) or *do-gi* ("suit of the way"). If the club does sell these items, ask how much these would cost.

Ask the students of the club what they think of their training. If you are happy with all the answers you receive, you may wish to enroll or start at that particular club.

Above: A good club—one where you feel confident in the teaching and are good friends with the members—can make all the difference in your karate training. Don't be afraid to ask questions before you join, and if possible, try out a couple of different clubs on a trial basis to find the one that suits you best.

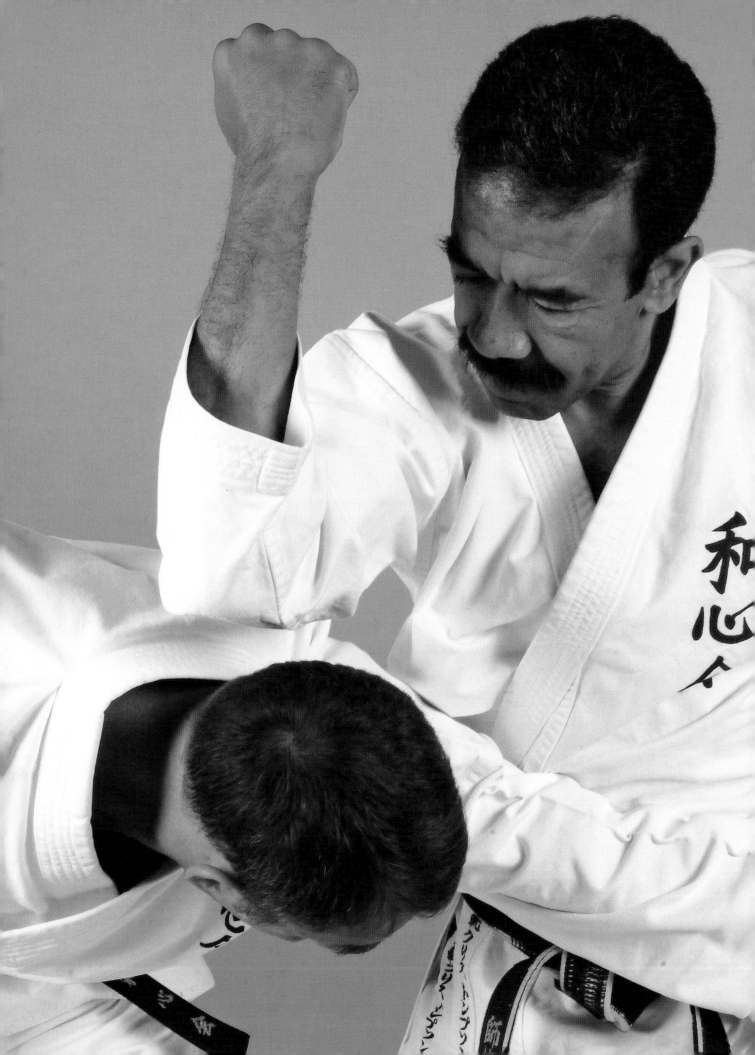

A short history of karate

Documented evidence of systematic fighting can be traced back over thousands of years in various cultures. The Egyptians carved hieroglyphics depicting fighting scenes into the walls of the pyramids, and a systematic form of unarmed combat was used in the early Greek Olympic Games, when fights often resulted in death. While the rest of the known world still lived in caves, China's advanced civilization also had a systematic form of unarmed fighting.

An Indian Buddhist monk named Bodhidharma (or Daruma in Japanese), usually credited with being the founder of Zen, is said to have traveled from India to China between the years AD 530 and 540. Here he settled at the Shaolin Temple, where he is accredited with introducing exercises to the monks, who were unfit and grossly overweight. These exercises would be classed as kung fu, or wushu, and are the foundation of today's modern karate. Unfortunately, there are some disagreements and discrepancies over this story, so I will give a short history of karate up to the present day using only documented and indisputable facts.

The island of Okinawa is the largest of the Ryukyu Islands found at the southern tip of Japan. Okinawa lies due east of China and is equidistant to Japan and the Chinese mainland. Throughout the centuries, the island's loyalties have been divided between Japan and China, both of which tried to colonize it. Okinawa's location also led to it becoming an important trading post for many countries of the Far East that were unable to trade with each other, either because of wars or the politics of the day. The island became a haven for seamen of many different nationalities who, by the very nature of their profession, were extremely tough and hardened men. They frequently exchanged their own peculiar fighting methods with one another in a friendly atmosphere, often while drinking, but it was not uncommon for these techniques to be exchanged in real combat. The Okinawans used all this invaluable knowledge to form their own eclectic fighting system.

During the fifteenth and sixteenth centuries, Chinese military attachés were based in Okinawa, as the two countries then had very strong ties. In the early seventeenth century, the Satsuma clan of Japan invaded Okinawa, forcing the islanders to capitulate rapidly. Okinawa was now in effect a colony under the direct rule of the Japanese. The everday routine of the Okinawans was uninterrupted; however, all weapons were now confiscated, making the islanders totally subservient. Confiscation of weapons had taken place earlier in Okinawa's history (in 1429), when the king's edict had insisted that the people could be motivated by education rather than traditional combat. Only high-ranking government officials and officers were permitted to carry weapons.

Even though Japan now controlled Okinawa, the islanders did not sever their links with the Chinese. Several Chinese military attachés were still allowed to live on the island and secretly taught the Okinawans forms of self-defense. This was called "chuan fa," or Chinese "fist way." The Chinese helped the Okinawans to merge

Left: The execution of *empi* (elbow strike) on the nape of an opponent's neck after avoiding his attack.
Below: *Uchi uke* (inside block)—blocking in and down with the left forearm, going completely past the body.

their primitive form of unarmed combat mentioned previously with a much more formalized style of unarmed combat. The fighting system that the Okinawans had developed themselves used all parts of their bodies, and was generally known as "Okinawan *te*" or "*tode*." Despite the secrecy shrouding *tode*, many began to study the art at an early age, learning from immediate family members or very close friends.

The three main towns on Okinawa—Shuri, Tomari, and Naha—created their own particular forms of Okinawan *te*. This led to the use of oft-heard phrases: "*shuri-te*," "*tomari-te*," and "*naha-te*," which described these forms (*te* meaning "hand"). *Shuri-te* became *shorin-ryu*, concentrating on faster execution of techniques with emphasis on speed, rather than strength. So over the centuries, via visiting Chinese military attachés, monks, seamen, and traders, a primitive form of indigenous Okinawan unarmed fighting evolved.

Above: The attacker kicks with a high roundhouse kick to the head (*mawashigeri jodan migi*). The defender leans back and blocks with his right forearm.

At the beginning of the twentieth century, the Russo-Japanese war was in progress and Japan conscripted heavily from Okinawa. An extremely alert Japanese army doctor noticed the unusually well-proportioned and strong physiques of many Okinawan conscripts. Investigations revealed that such physiques were due to the practice of *te*. Japanese officials on Okinawa approved the inclusion of *te* in the physical curriculum of Okinawan schools in 1902 because they could see the military advantages of such a system, which could be used for conditioning future soldiers. Eventually *te* became known as "*karate-jutsu*," the ideogram of which means "Chinese hand art."

The then Crown Prince Hirohito, touring Okinawa, witnessed a demonstration of karate-jutsu and was so favorably impressed that he included the event in his formal report to the Japanese government, which led to the Minister of Education inviting an Okinawan expert to Japan. The person chosen was Gichin Funakoshi. Funakoshi was selected not because the Okinawans felt that he was the best exponent of the art of *te*, but rather because he was a primary school teacher and his Japanese was very good. He also came from a family with a good background, which was essential if he was to gain any credibility at all with the Japanese.

It is interesting to note that Funakoshi, hoping to establish karate on the main island of Japan a lot earlier, had made an exploratory visit to the Japanese mainland in 1917 and given a demonstration of Okinawan *te* to officials from the upper classes. Unfortunately, this meant that all spectators were from the upper classes or aristocracy, descendants of the samurai. To them, karate was nothing more than a set of exercises for street fighting without weapons, fit only for a plebeian class of people. Members of the aristocracy felt that any form of combat that did not use a sword was inferior. In addition, the Japanese were reluctant to accept any type of combat that had not been developed directly on the mainland island; if it came from an island such as Okinawa, it was automatically deemed inferior.

On Funakoshi's second visit to Japan in 1922, however, his display was open to the public, at the first sports festival held in Tokyo. Funakoshi and Okinawan *te*, or karate-jutsu, proved an immediate success, and before long their great popularity among the young Japanese, especially university students, gave this art a larger following in Japan than it enjoyed in Okinawa. Funakoshi quickly struck up a relationship with Jigoro Kano, the founder of modern-day judo. After many discussions, he adopted a style of uniform, *gi*, very similar

Above: The attacker throws a left reverse punch to the body (*gyakuzuki chudan hidari*). The defender blocks with a left palm heel (*hidari teisho uke*).

to that worn by the judo exponents. He also adopted Kano's system of awarding black belts ("*dan*") to his senior students after a formal assessment. This would prove invaluable, as it was one of the stipulations that the Dai Nippon Butokukai (the Japanese body for controlling martial arts) required from prospective candidates.

In 1931, karate was accepted into the Butokukai, under the stipulation that the following conditions were met: the word "karate" was written in Japanese characters and not Chinese; karate-do adopted a standard uniform; a form of tournament was held regularly; and the black-belt system was instituted.

Still, the rapid proliferation of Japanese karate-jutsu cannot be credited to the teachings of Gichin Funakoshi alone. Many skilled exponents have influenced the formation of Japanese karate-do and have shared in promoting its growth.

The growth of karate

From the traditionalist point of view, Funakoshi must be considered the father of Japanese karate-do, as it is he who was responsible for making many important innovations to karate-jutsu and who brought this Okinawan art to the Japanese and, later, the Western world.

In 1933, Funakoshi changed the concept of "kara," which was originally written with the Chinese character meaning "China hand," by substituting another character for "kara," signifying "void" or "empty." Therefore, the new karate-jutsu developed by Funakoshi meant "empty." Two years later, Funakoshi discarded the word "jutsu" in favor of the word "do" ("the way of"). Thus, karate-do (along the lines of ju-do and aiki-do) was born in Japan. The literal meaning is "empty hand way," emphasizing the lack of weapons in this fighting art.

The beginnings of Shotokan

Funakoshi established a central dojo (training hall) in Tokyo in 1936. After deliberating, he gave it the name "Shotokan." He did not pick this name himself; it was thrust upon him by his students. The "shoto" ideogram was Funakoshi's pen name as a calligrapher. The "kan" ideogram meant "hall." This was to be the "honbu" (headquarters) of his karate organization: the Shotokan.

World War II saw karate-jutsu, or karate-do, become officially recognized as a valuable part of the training process of the Japanese military, both soldiers and sailors. The mass participation of Japan's young men resulted in the rapid growth of new unarmed karate techniques. Even after the Japanese defeat, when most martial arts were prohibited as they were considered to foster militarism, karate systems continued to flourish. Just as the Okinawans practiced their *te* in secret after being invaded by the Satsuma clan, similarly, the Japanese practiced their karate-do after the end of World War II. With the banning of any form of military exercise or martial art, karate could not be practiced openly. This hidden form of training continued until the ban was lifted on all forms of martial art in 1952.

By the very early 1950s, when all the bans had been lifted, the technical progress of karate-do had increased tremendously. The styles of karate that had been established before the outbreak of World War II now began to flourish, and a syllabus for all the various styles that were being practiced began to be developed. Senior experts of several *ryu* (schools) established a national body for the new martial arts schools to ensure that high standards were maintained. This, in turn, led to far greater numbers of high school and university students entering karate-do competitions, making it an art of both popular appeal and national importance.

Funakoshi had specific ideas in mind when he replaced the character for "kara," which had meant "China hand," with the modern character meaning "empty." The fact that Japanese karate-do does not involve the use the weapons, only parts of the body, gives literal meaning to the translation. Many traditionalists in Okinawa were angered by this change because of its

Above: *Hidari gyakuzuki chudan*—left mid-section reverse punch—a technique practiced by every student who studies karate.

obvious conflict with the original Okinawan systems on which karate-do is based. These systems always included the use of specific weapons: *bo* (a six-foot long staff), *nunchuku* (rice flails), *tonfa* (rice-grinding flails), *sai* (large metal-pronged forks), *kama* (sickles), and *tekko* (metal knuckle-dusters). Funakoshi clarified the apparent paradox and gained much support from his fellow Okinawans by declaring that the use of the ideogram "empty" was based on the concept of unselfishness. Thus, the emptiness suggested by the newly chosen character referred to the state of rendering oneself empty or egoless. Funakoshi stressed that he taught karate as an exercise for the mind and body that built personal character.

Spreading popularity

During the American armed forces' occupation of Japan after World War II, Westerners gained their first sight of karate-do. Many US servicemen found the exercises and drills carried out by the Japanese ex-servicemen fascinating—so much so that they wanted to join in and find out what the Japanese were doing. These US servicemen became early members of Japanese karate-do. Although there was resentment toward foreigners in the classes, the Japanese had no option but to teach the Westerners (*gaijin*), fearing that rejection of the new students would result in the closure of classes and an obvious loss of income, and therefore the art. Once accepted by the Japanese, the US servicemen were taught the finer points of karate-do, making it possible for their knowledge to be passed on when they were posted back to the United States.

The goal of many Japanese instructors was to see their art flourish worldwide, and they could see the benefits of teaching Americans. Indeed, many Americans did set about teaching this strange new art of karate-do upon their return to the United States, and thus karate was introduced to Americans in the early 1950s. With Japanese and American trade expanding rapidly after the war, many senior Japanese *karate-ka* (one who practices karate) visited the United States and some settled there permanently. Today, every style of Japanese karate has a school somewhere in the United States, and practitioners number many thousands.

A worldwide practice

A Frenchman called Henri Plee is credited with introducing karate to Europe, in 1957. Plee is acknowledged as being the first person to bring a Japanese expert in karate-do to Europe from Japan.

The person credited with first bringing karate-do to the United Kingdom was Vernon Bell, who trained under Plee in Paris, and later brought over Japanese experts, such as Kanazawa *sensei*, a Shotokan stylist from Japan. By the mid-1960s, the demand for karate was so great worldwide that many Japanese karate-ka were invited to numerous countries to teach on a permanent basis, as it was felt that the standard of karate-do needed to be raised. As a result, there are Japanese instructors resident around the world, especially in the styles of Shotokan, Wado-ryu, Goju-ryu, and Shito-ryu.

Today, it seems as if there is not a country in the world that does not have at least one karate club. In the past 50 years, the popularity of this art has attracted millions of people from every walk of life. Funakoshi could never have dreamed that his beloved art would leave his small island of Okinawa and be studied and taught by people of every race.

Styles of karate

Funakoshi was not the only Okinawan to bring karate to mainland Japan. Many of his compatriots whose roots and tutors were different from those of Funakoshi were also responsible for bringing the sport to Japan.

Chojun Miyagi (1888–1953) brought the style of Goju-ryu karate to Japan, along with Kenwa Mabuni (1889–1952), who brought the style of Shito-ryu karate to the mainland. Kanban Uechi (1877–1948) was another Okinawan who left his home to teach his form of karate to the Japanese. He had studied martial arts in China at the end of the nineteenth century and stayed in that country for approximately 13 years before returning to Okinawa. In 1924, Uechi went to Japan to teach his style of martial arts, and by 1940 had decided to name his style Uechi-ryu karate. His style of karate never gained the popularity of Funakoshi's, Miyagi's, or Mabuni's, however, and he returned to Okinawa in 1947. It was only after his death, one year later, that Uechi-ryu style became very popular in his native Okinawa. Kanban Uechi's son continued to teach the style after his father's death, but the style never grew and expanded at the rate that Kanban Uechi had desired.

Many of the Okinawans who brought their karate to Japan were not openly accepted. In addition, they found it hard to settle into the Japanese way of life and decided to return home. Those that were fortunate enough to stay and prosper have left their mark on the world of karate-do. Today, there are hundreds of styles worldwide, but the vast majority can trace their roots back to the handful of Okinawan pioneers who decided to share their knowledge with the rest of the world in the first half of the twentieth century.

Shotokan karate

Gichin Funakoshi (1868–1957), already acknowledged as the founder of modern-day karate, was reluctant to call his style a *ryu* (school)—he simply labeled it "karate-do." His teachings in the 1930s differed greatly from his contemporaries in Okinawa and from the way he himself was taught. He had a profound effect on all his students and placed much emphasis on their mental awareness, alongside developing physical prowess.

The Shotokan that we are familiar with today can be credited more to Funakoshi's third son, who was known affectionately as Giko. He, like

Hironori Ohtsuka, founder of the Wado-ryu style of karate, believed in applying karate techniques in actual free fighting. As with all young men of that generation, he wanted to test his skills on someone else. By 1936, when Gichin Funakoshi established a Shotokan school of karate in Tokyo, he was already a 68-year-old man. Even though he had a tremendous following, a lot of the burden was now placed on his son. The young Funakoshi's style of karate was quite different from that of his father's. The older Funakoshi had always adopted high stances; those of his son were a lot lower. His son also used full leg extension techniques such as *mawashigeri* (roundhouse kick) and *yoko-geri* (side kick), which he is credited with introducing into karate. The *kata* of Shotokan are numerous and some even have derivations, which reflect the older Funakoshi's teachings. Today, Shotokan is the style of karate that is most practiced throughout the world.

Left: A movement from an advanced Shotokan *kata enpi*.
Below: A movement from a *hente waza* sequence—blocking and countering an attack with the same limb.

Wado-ryu karate—a Japanese style of karate

The founder of Wado-ryu karate, Hironori Ohtsuka (1892–1982), was born on June 1, 1892 in Shimodate City, Ibaraki prefecture, Japan. By the time he was six years of age, he had already started training in ju jitsu, studying under his maternal great-uncle. Upon entering middle school at the age of 13, he started to study Shindo Yoshin-ryu ju jitsu under Tatsusaboro Nakayama. These studies continued with Nakayama throughout his education at Waseda University, resulting in Ohtsuka being awarded his *menkyo* (license-level proficiency) in Shindo Yoshin-ryu under Nakayama in 1921.

In 1922, Ohtsuka heard of the karate demonstration given by Gichin Funakoshi in Tokyo and was determined to meet him. Throughout his studies of ju jitsu, Ohtsuka always sought out other styles of ju jitsu, trying to visit as many different dojo as possible. Ohtsuka could not contain his excitement at the advent of a completely new, weaponless martial art. He met Funakoshi at his residence, the Meisei Juku, a boarding house for Okinawan students, in the same year. They talked for several hours, discussing their interpretations of the martial arts, and by the end of that evening, Funakoshi agreed to accept Ohtsuka as a student at his karate dojo. Ohtsuka started training with Funakoshi immediately, and his enthusiasm and martial arts background meant that he quickly grasped the physical techniques that he was being taught. In just over a year, he had studied and knew the movements of every single *kata* (form) that Funakoshi had taught him. *Kata* was the only aspect of karate that Funakoshi taught at that time. Throughout this period, Ohtsuka did not cease his training in ju jitsu and began to incorporate this into his karate jutsu. In April 1924, Ohtsuka, aged 31, along with six others, was graded to black belt by Funakoshi. He thus became one of the first Japanese black belts in karate-do.

The continued devotion of Ohtsuka to ju jitsu and karate-do

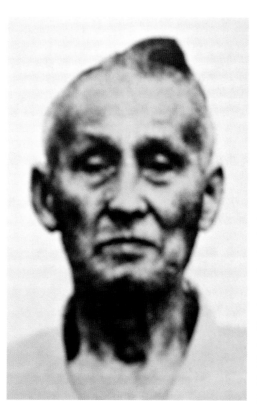

Above: Hironori Ohtsuka (1892–1982), founder of Wado-ryu karate.

led to Ohtsuka becoming a *shihan* (Grand Master) of Shindo Yoshin-ryu and Funakoshi's assistant instructor. He also began to train with other famous martial artists, such as Kenwa Mabuni, founder of the Shito-ryu style, and Choki Motobu, famed as a fighter in karate. As a proficient karate instructor, Ohtsuka began teaching at Tokyo University and his methods began to conflict with Funakoshi's teachings. Ohtsuka's brand of karate incorporated his ju jitsu techniques, enabling his students to practice free sparring. This was not to Funakoshi's liking and, as his concept of karate differed greatly from Ohtsuka's, Funakoshi felt that actual fighting, *jissen*, was far too dangerous and would immediately result in the death of one of the participants. On the other hand, Ohtsuka believed that, with specific guidance and rules, the students could use techniques in free fighting without severe injury. Ohtsuka's departure from Funakoshi was inevitable.

Goju-ryu karate

Goju-ryu, meaning "hard-soft school," was founded by the Okinawan Chojun Miyagi, one of a few students of the great Kannryo Higoanna, a *naha-te* karate instructor. Miyagi studied with him until Higoanna's death in 1915, then traveled to China to continue his studies of various forms of *wushu*, a Chinese martial art. Upon his return to Okinawa, he merged his *wushu* teachings (soft) with his *naha-te* teachings (hard). He took the name "Goju" from a passage in the *Bubishi* (a handwritten book passed down from one generation of martial artists to the next). Like other Okinawans who were extremely competent, Miyagi was asked to teach his Goju style in Japan. He traveled from the island of Okinawa to Kyoto and other cities in the southern half of Japan, but found himself extremely homesick. Gogen Yamaguchi was one of his last Japanese disciples and, before he returned to Okinawa, Miyagi passed Yamaguchi the mantle, letting him become his senior disciple in Japan. Yamaguchi created a different style of Goju. The fundamentals were still there, but he gave it more of a Japanese influence and we now have two forms of Goju-ryu karate: Goju-ryu and Goju-kai. Yamaguchi placed a great deal of emphasis on internal strength. Both forms of Goju are well represented worldwide.

Shito-ryu karate

The founder of Shito-ryu was Kenwa Mabuni, an Okinawan like Funakoshi, who had Kannryo Higoanna as his instructor, the same man who instructed Chojun Miyagi, the founder of Goju-ryu, as well as Anko Itosu, one of Funakoshi's instructors. This gave Mabuni a chance to practice *naha-te*-style karate, as well as *shuri-te*-style karate. Therefore, he covered *naha, shuri,* and *tomari kata.* Being a close friend of Miyagi, Mabuni also visited China with him to study the Chinese *wushu* forms. With such an amassed amount of knowledge, Mabuni created a style based on more than 60 *kata,* and called it Hanko-ryu.

Above: Kenwa Mabuni (1889–1952), founder of Shito-ryu karate.

He eventually changed the name to Shito-ryu, which was an amalgamation of the names of two instructors who had taught him: Itosu and Higoanna (Chinese characters). Like Funakoshi, Mabuni traveled to Japan in the late 1920s and settled in the southern area of the country near Osaka, where he taught his Shito-ryu. It is very popular in Japan and now, through competition, very popular on the tournament circuit, both inside and outside of Japan.

Kyokushinkai karate

Kyokushinkai was founded by Matsutatsu Oyama (1923–1994). Even though it is not one of the four original main styles of karate, it is still very popular both in Japan and worldwide.

Matsutatsu Oyama, a Korean-born and naturalized Japanese, developed Kyokushinkai, "school of ultimate truth" (a style that was as close to combat as one could get). Its concepts of *ikken hisatsu* (one punch, one kick technique) to stop an opponent are the foundation of the style. This is why it immediately became very popular with the Japanese. Oyama was influenced by both

Funakoshi of Shotokan and Yamaguchi of Goju-kai, but found that neither of the styles of these men could convey the true combative spirit for which he was looking. After a self-imposed period of isolation away from the city and the limelight, Oyama re-emerged to demonstrate his own style of karate by fighting bulls bare-handed, successfully killing three, each with a single blow. This gave him immediate popularity—and having a cartoon strip in a national magazine also highlighted his fame. At one stage his style was one of the fastest-growing karate schools in the world. Since his death, however, the Kyokushinkai organization has shrunk, although the style is still practiced.

Its popularity is largely due to the dynamic actions of the techniques, and it appeals to spectators in the same way that gladiators in the Colosseum of ancient Rome did to the Romans. Toward the end of his life, Oyama spent a lot of his time organizing knock-down tournaments that relied on an opponent being knocked down to determine the winner. This made it easy for spectators to see who had won and who had lost. His style proudly boasts of being extremely hard and unrelenting in its training. This type of tournament is deemed "full contact."

The karate basics

The three fundamental areas of karate training are called *kihon*, *kata,* and *kumite*. All three must be practiced diligently, with equal time allotted to each one. They are interlinked, and each aspect of the training elements helps the others. The physical practice of these three elements of karate do more than just hone the technical skills that are required by karate practitioners—they also help the mental training of all karate students.

Karate-ka also train to attain a level of *mushin*, an involuntary reaction to attack, where there is no thought process in the execution of technique and the movements are done instinctively. It may only be avoidance from an attack, e.g. sidestepping or ducking away, without the necessity to retaliate in any way whatsoever. If action is required, there will be no hesitancy in using the correct karate technique for the given situation. This level of achievement cannot be gained without many years of diligent, regular training in *kihon*, *kata,* and *kumite*, hence their importance.

It is extremely repetitive training and because of this, the *sensei* must be inspirational with their tuition. Motivation is a major requirement to get the students back in the dojo day after day, week after week. When the level of black belt is achieved, the student should realize just how important their study of *kihon*, *kata,* and *kumite* has been to them.

Kihon (basic technique)

In *kihon* training, which is the practice of fundamental basic techniques, students are taught to strengthen their punching, kicking, and blocking regularly, with much repetition, refining, and honing of techniques. *Kihon* covers combinations as well as individual techniques, and this encompasses strikes, punches, and kicks. It is essential to grasp the fundamentals before you can advance in karate. Students are taught, regardless of style, to try to stop the opponent with one technique. This is still the ideal training goal, as it focuses the mind and aims to increase the *kime* (focused power) in each technique delivered while training.

Combination techniques also come under *kihon* practice. These are where two attacks are put together. One kick, one punch; or two kicks, two punches; or several combinations of all while moving forward in a dojo is practicing your *kihon* technique.

No matter what technique you deliver, you must always visualize your opponent while practicing your *kihon*. Always train to keep full control of your body, placing your feet and hand techniques accurately at the imaginary target. Speed is essential, along with good posture, balance, and breathing. Always complete your techniques, whether they are single or combinations, with a strong *kiai* (a loud shout in which all energy is expelled) at the end.

Unfortunately, because of the repetitive nature of *kihon* techniques, after a while many students become disillusioned and leave karate. This is a shame, as many potentially good *karate-ka* quit at an early stage. This tends to happen only to beginners who do not have any

Left: Practicing the basic punch of karate to body mid-section level—*hidari chudan tsuki*.
Below: The fighter on the left performs a *gyakuzuki chudan* (reverse punch) with the left fist in a bout of *ji-yu kumite* (free fighting).

concept of what this basic repetitive training is doing for them physically and mentally. The Japanese adopt a completely different attitude toward *kihon* training. They realize that a house can only be built upon a solid foundation. A minimum of 30 minutes should be devoted to *kihon* training in any one session.

It is during this sort of rigorous training that strong technique is developed, especially on your weaker side. Performing up to 500 repetitions of a single technique is not uncommon, and can only be beneficial both mentally and physically. Maintaining the posture and keeping the limb up during such practice is demanding. If you are not in a class being tutored, the main aid for the solitary practice of *kihon* is a mirror. This will assist with correction of technique.

Correct *kokyu* (breathing) is essential when carrying out any maneuver in karate, and this can also be perfected in *kihon* training. Always remember to expel the air in the body when exerting yourself, especially through a *kiai*. Never carry out strenuous technique without taking in good quantities of air. It is through *kihon* training that all the other aspects of your karate will improve.

Kata (form, or pattern of movement)

Practicing *kata* teaches students many different fighting techniques. *Kata*, or form, is a prearranged sequence of techniques delivering strikes, punches, and kicks, performed by an individual, like a dance routine. In fact, there is strong evidence that a form of *kata*, more like a dance, existed in Okinawa long before China had a controlling influence there.

When looking at different Chinese systems and training with Chinese martial arts instructors, it is quite obvious that there are great similarities in both execution of techniques and application. It is well known that Okinawan *te* was greatly influenced by the Chinese military fighting systems.

Modern karate-do still has *kata* as its backbone. Karate is *kata* training. If no *kata* is practiced in karate training, one is not really practicing it—*kata* is the life and soul of karate. In *kata* training, you strive to focus the mind on imaginary attacks and counter-attacks, and simultaneously let the body carry out the physical actions, making the mind and body one.

Advanced *kata* are practiced in exactly the same way as basic *kata*, methodically and deliberately, while ensuring that the subject matter is completely learned and understood. As well as picking up the physical techniques, it is useful to learn the history of the *kata*, if at all

possible. The *bunkai* (application of the *kata* techniques) is extremely important, and the *kata* cannot be understood if the *bunkai* is not explained.

Always practice *kata* slowly initially, until confidence is gained, then apply speed and power to your techniques. Concentrate on the rhythm of the movements, making sure the combinations are fast and powerful, and the slow movements are deliberate and purposeful. In the captions and photographs illustrating examples throughout this book, I have shown where these changes of rhythm take place. Always remember that the *kata* illustrated throughout the book are only guides, but they will aid your karate training.

You can never learn *kata* solely from a book, film, or DVD. There is absolutely no substitute for a good *sensei* (teacher, or, literally, "one who has been before"). A *sensei* can help to inspire good performance and motivate you with good, clear instruction. What's more, without good, regular instruction, there is always the tendency to improvise when uncertain about the next movement in *kata*; this can establish a pattern of errors that can then become ingrained. This unfortunately happens all too often and has seen the loss of many of the true movements of numerous historical *kata*.

Gaining a feeling of satisfaction with every performance of a *kata* is rare, if not impossible, but this must simply be accepted as part of your practice, and not be seen as a negative.

Ji-yu kumite (free fighting; nothing prearranged)

Ji-yu kumite is an essential part of karate training and also a *karate-ka*'s development. Emphasis must be placed upon *ji-yu kumite* at all levels of a student's progress, starting with simple techniques and building up degrees of difficulty. Initially, the fear of fighting, regardless of how tame it is, must be overcome; this is a major obstacle for some students. This is one of the reasons why I stated at the beginning of this chapter that equal training time must be given to all aspects: *kihon*, *kata,* and *kumite*.

Kumite, although considered dangerous by some, can be most enjoyable to practice. Pitting one's wits against an opponent is invigorating and challenging. Karate is a martial art and certain techniques are far too dangerous to use in *ji-yu kumite* practice, and are therefore prohibited. Examples of these are open-hand strikes to the face; strikes to the joints (*kansetsu-waza*); groin strikes; and punching or striking at vulnerable targets, such as the carotid artery, the nape of the neck, and the small of the back (lower spine). Nevertheless, there are many techniques (*waza*) that can be used while practicing your *ji-yu kumite*. Beside basic skills such as kicks (*keri*) and punches (*tsuki*), there are strikes (*uchi*), hip shifts (*taisabaki*), flowing, body shifting (*nagashi*), evasion (*kawashi*), entering (*irimi*), and escaping (*nogare*) to be practiced. Practicing *ji-yu kumite* at other clubs and with other students of different styles is also beneficial for your advancement.

Competition is a major way of practicing *ji-yu kumite*. There are restrictions on the techniques that can be delivered in competition, however, unlike in the dojo where pretty much everything is allowed, with control being the key for safety. Obviously, your skills will improve with practice. As you climb the ladder of advancement, whether it is through gradings or in time, you will find a great improvement in your well-being.

The main ingredients for successful application in *ji-yu kumite* are the same as in *kihon* and *kata*: speed, timing, distance, accuracy and, above all, confidence in the application of technique. Overconfidence, however, can work against you. As your confidence builds, it is quite easy to become totally immersed in *ji-yu kumite* practice, and what seems like five minutes of sparring often turns out to be an hour's session. You become totally absorbed and involved in what you are doing. To be proficient in *ji-yu kumite* alone, in my opinion, does not make a good, true *karate-ka*. A rounded *karate-ka* practices *kihon*, *kata*, and *kumite*, and it usually shows in the person's demeanor.

The Japanese maxim "*shin gi tai*" (unite your mind, body, and spirit) is used by *sensei* when explaining the fundamentals of karate to students, especially in hard, demanding classes of *kihon*, *kata*, or *kumite*.

SHU-HA-RI

The term *shu-ha-ri* is often heard in karate, as well as in many other Japanese martial arts, but it is very rarely understood. *Shu-ha-ri* is what all students of karate strive to achieve, but the philosophy of *shu-ha-ri* can be applied to all walks of life.

- **First stage of training (*shu*):** The student follows the *sensei*'s instructions completely, obeying every command, in order to learn the *waza* (techniques)—every aspect of the *sensei*'s tuition must be followed diligently.
- **Second stage of training (*ha*):** With this continuous training, the second stage, *ha,* is aimed for, where the student tries to be better than the *sensei* with more accomplished *waza*.
- **Final stage of training (*ri*):** The final stage, *ri*, where, after learning from the *sensei*, obeying every instruction, the student feels he or she has surpassed the *sensei*, thus completing the circle.

Shu-ha-ri can only be obtained, however, if the student's character has developed along with his or her technique.

Right: Performing a right *jodan uraken uchi* and left *zenwan munemae kamae* in *jion kata* ("temple ground" pattern of movement).

What is a black belt?

A *dan* grade (black belt) in karate is awarded to a student who has achieved an advanced level of proficiency in the art, usually through a physical test. *Kyu* level (indicated by the colored belts) shows a level of competence in the art, but is far below that which is required for *dan* level.

To have obtained a black belt, a student will have proven that they are a competent martial artist capable of defending themselves against an unarmed attacker, or even an armed attacker. They must be able to use all their limbs as effective weapons. By the time a student has achieved a black belt, they will also have an understanding of all techniques that make up a true fighting system, e.g. strikes, locks, punches, kicks, chokes, holds, and throws.

Karate students are assessed on their ability to deliver techniques effectively, hence a physical examination. However, being a black belt does not make a student invincible—it will not help if you are attacked with a metal bar to the back of the head, for instance, and ten-year-old black belts may be competent but will still be disadvantaged both physically and mentally due to their youth. For this reason, an age restriction should be in place before one is allowed a black belt. Maturity is a quality that comes only with experience of life. How can this possibly be attained by someone of very young age? Children may have physical prowess, but if they burst into tears when intimidated, how can they justify calling themselves a black belt in karate? The failing here lies with either the *sensei* or examiner in promoting them, but be wary of any dojo that encourages such practices.

The mere fact of having achieved black-belt status demonstrates that the person is competent and has achieved a certain recognized standard, but it is just the first rung on the ladder of learning. The other major aspect of achieving the goal of becoming a *yudansha* (black belt level) is the personality and character of a student. Someone with a belligerent demeanor would, through rigorous training, have thrown off that aspect of their personality by black belt level, and achieved some measure of equanimity and mastery over their emotions. If this development does not take place, the examining authority would be unlikely to accept that person as a *yudansha* candidate. In this way, body and mind must develop together and at the right pace.

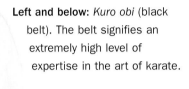

Left and below: *Kuro obi* (black belt). The belt signifies an extremely high level of expertise in the art of karate.

Gichin Funakoshi was the first karate *sensei* to issue his students with a *dan*-grade rank. He copied the system that Jigoro Kano (the founder of modern-day judo) had created. Initially, a black sash was awarded, but this changed to a thicker black belt (*kuro obi*) when the *gi* (white uniform) was introduced to karate. Funakoshi made it abundantly clear that to receive a karate shodan (first level of black belt) meant that the student was at the beginning of a new phase in their training and not at the end.

This system continues worldwide today, and the *dan* ranking usually varies between five and ten *dan* levels. One's proficiency in the art is acknowledged with the higher number of *dan* levels.

When will I get my black belt?

This is what a lot of people ask when they start karate training, or are halfway up the ladder of *kyu* grades (the stages before first black belt, or *shodan*): how long is it going to take? This depends on commitment, how long and how often you train, and what progress is made.

It is quite often said that there are two stages of karate. Until you reach *shodan*, or first black belt, you are literally a beginner. It is at *shodan* level that you study karate and really begin to learn. As you go up the *kyu* steps, a lot of skills are learned, and by the time you get to black belt you should be a competent and confident person, able to look after yourself, and mentally you will have gained some wisdom. One hopes!

Criteria for obtaining a black belt

This is achieved by continuous and regular training, along with following and obeying your *sensei* in everything you are instructed to do. Your *sensei* will not just watch and correct your physical movements; he will also observe your character and demeanor. It is not just prowess with karate technique that makes one a good black belt; it is also the mental training.

By whom are you recognized?

We all want to know that, when we receive our black belt, it is a recognized qualification. All those hours, months, and years of hard physical and mental training should be acknowledged and accepted by the governing authorities of karate.

No matter what country karate is practiced in, the governing body is called the World Karate Federation (WKF), and it has more than 15 million practitioners on its books. These members are from countries around the globe, and the WKF is recognized by the

International Olympic Committee (IOC). Still, even though karate has IOC recognition, it is not included in the Olympic Games at present, despite hopes for its acceptance. We can only hope that karate will be an official Olympic sport at some stage in the future.

Nonetheless, as it is recognized by the IOC as a sport, it is very important to verify that your club belongs to the WKF, whether through the club, association, or group, in order to have your gradings ratified.

Above: *Yudansha* (black belt level) is not merely achieved by physical prowess—your psychological strength is just as important and should not be neglected.

Competition karate

There have been several forms of competition rules used in karate over the past few decades, but the two that have remained consistent are the Shobu Ippon rules and, more recently, the WKF (World Karate Federation) rules.

Competition training is a vital part of most karate clubs. It is essential to let students test their skills in competition; it also helps them to fight their inhibitions. Obviously, they should be allowed to compete only against students who possess the same level of competence. Some karate clubs still believe, however, that competition is far too dangerous and therefore they do not encourage students to participate in it at all.

Shobu Ippon competition

Shobu Ippon is the original form of competition, and was used in Japan before being exported to the rest of the world in the 1950s. It is deemed a realistic form of competition, even with its strict rules regarding safety. The scoring is simple, with a *wazari* (half point) being given by the referee for a technique that is deemed powerful enough to damage or wound, but not enough to kill. An *ippon* (one point) is awarded by the referee for a technique that is deemed strong enough to kill. The competition match is won when the fighter has achieved an *ippon* score. This situation can happen within a few

KARATE NI SENTENASHI

The meaning of the phrase "*karate ni sentenashi*," which is commonly known to most *karate-ka*, is that a *karate-ka* must never attack first, either physically or mentally. As a *karate-ka* grows in stature, through constant and regular training, good manners will become evident along with humility. After many years of rigorous training and correct dojo etiquette, the *karate-ka* will fully understand the significance of "*karate ni sentenashi*."

Left: The attacker kicks with a hooking reverse roundhouse to the head (*ura mawashi-geri jodan*).
Right: The attacker on the left throws a left *mawashi-geri jodan* (roundhouse kick to the head). She forces the defender around by adjusting her position.

seconds of the bout commencing. Two *wazari* scores will end a match immediately. If, at the end of the allotted time of the bout, one competitor has a *wazari*, then that competitor will be the winner.

This system, with its various rules, is still seen by many practitioners of karate as the most realistic form of competition. The reasoning is that it reflects the true spirit of *budo* (realistic fighting of the samurai). Therefore the traditionalists insist that, if competition is going to take place, it should be under these rules and not those of the WKF. Traditionalists think that the WKF system is far too unrealistic, with its continuous scoring of "weak techniques."

Above: As the attacker (on the left) punches to the body, the defender blocks with a left *gedan barai* and delivers a right *uraken* strike to the side of the face.

WKF competition

The WKF rules for competition karate are far more detailed than that of Shobu Ippon. Scoring is rewarded with *ippon* (one point), *nihon* (two points), and *sanbon* (three points).

Dynamic varied technique is encouraged, with high kicks to make it attractive to spectators and, above all, extreme control of *waza* to avoid any serious injury. The WKF rules are there to encourage a more sporting element to karate, but not to the detriment of good technique. Fitness, strength, and good *waza* are still paramount under the WKF rules.

The debate between Shobu Ippon and WKF rules has been going on for years, but many competitors compete in both Shobu Ippon and WKF competitions. As an example, Shotokan stylists, who generally stick to Shobu Ippon competition, will often compete under WKF rules if they wish to represent their club or association, or even their country.

If *karate-ka* wish to compete and be involved in WKF competitions that are IOC-recognized, then they must learn and study the WKF rules.

REISHIKI (DOJO DISCIPLINE)

Any area or space in which a *karate-ka* trains becomes, in spirit, a dojo. A *karate-ka* must at all times show correct etiquette toward fellow students, their *sempai* (seniors), and their *sensei*. There should be no "orders" given—merely mutual respect and co-operation between *sensei* and *deshi* (pupil).

Discipline is more strict in a properly run dojo than in almost any other situation, yet the air is not repressive because this discipline is self-imposed. There are times when students may converse freely or even joke and laugh inside the dojo without breaking etiquette. The new karate student need only behave politely in order to be in accord with the correct spirit of etiquette.

Gasshuku

Most karate organizations hold a *gasshuku*, or extended training camp. They may be called summer camps or winter camps, but they are *gasshuku* if they are held away from the normal dojo and last for more than a day. The training at a *gasshuku* could be deemed as austere karate training. This is not because the training is extremely tough; it is because it lasts for several hours during the day, and continues the following day, and possibly the day after that. Many techniques are covered on these courses and *gasshuku* provide a chance to gain new knowledge in a short period.

A *gasshuku* can also be an occasion to meet old friends from other clubs whom you may not have seen for more than a year, especially if it is through an international organization. Obviously, it is a great time to make new friendships with *karate-ka* from different clubs. Instructors

Above: Students and tutors at a summer *gasshuku* enjoying the training and the cameraderie.
Below: Striking an opponent's leg in *ohyo gumite* or *yakusoku gumite*.

may also use this opportunity to meet and share experiences. *Gasshuku* can become very enjoyable social events.

Many karate groups use a *gasshuku* as a time to hold meetings or even an annual general meeting for their organizations. *Gasshuku* classes will usually be held outside on a level surface, weather permitting. Even though students and instructors leave the course fairly exhausted and with aching limbs, they always want to know the dates of the next *gasshuku*, and are eager to ensure that there will be a place for them the next time around.

Karate fundamentals

Karate, like many other physical sports, requires the body to function efficiently and correctly under all the heavy demands placed upon it. It is essential, therefore, that the body is warmed up before starting to practice and use the techniques of karate.

Through the continuous practice of basic techniques (*kihon*), the body becomes much stronger and and can be relied upon when using blocks, punches, strikes, and kicks. A high level of tenacity is developed at this stage, which assists with the mental training so vital to the sport.

Kata (form) practice must also be covered, enabling you to use your fighting skills against an imaginary opponent. Some movements in *kata* are slow and graceful, while others are extremely fast and powerful. No matter how these moves are delivered, they have a function that will be explained to you by your *sensei* as you progress.

Actual sparring (*ji yu kumite*) with another *karate-ka* will put all the elements of your karate training together. You will have diligently practiced your stances, punches, and kicks and you can now test your skills against another unarmed student.

These are the fundamentals of karate training. However, the ethos of karate is to strive to be a better person through your practice. Eventually you will discover that the toughest opponent you will ever face is yourself.

Left: The author helping students practice their techniques in class.

Rei (bowing at the beginning and end of a karate class)

All karate classes start and finish with a formal bow (*rei*). Many groups have an elaborate system in place, acknowledging all the seniors in the class (*sempai*), as well as the *sensei*, but the majority of classes make the formal bow a short affair lasting no more than two or three minutes. This is done out of respect to the instructor, the dojo, and all the fellow participants studying karate-do.

Dojo-kun

It is when the bowing takes place, either before a class starts, or when it is finishing that the *dojo-kun* will be shouted. The *dojo-kun* can be the philosophy of the organization, or the rules of the dojo to which everybody must adhere. Usually a senior or the *sensei* will call out the *dojo-kun*. Quite often the students will repeat the commands out loud. Once this has been done, the bows will take place.

1. Students prepare to drop into the bowing position.
2. Students bow to the *sensei*—"*Sensei ni rei.*"
3. Students bow to each other—"*Otagai ni rei.*"
4. The *dojo-kun* being recited.

Junbi undo (limbering up)

Getting the body warmed up before starting

It is very important that warming-up, cooling-down, and stretching exercises are carried out, not just for beginners in karate, but for all levels of student, especially advanced ones.

When warming up, calisthenic exercises (the same as gymnasts carry out) are key. They should be done systematically and regularly, with many repetitions. Some need to be done slowly and deliberately, while others are carried out quite rapidly. The body temperature should be raised through exercising and stretching, to prevent any injury occurring once you begin your karate session.

Deep stretching, especially for the legs, is necessary to improve flexibility and speed. This must be carried out carefully, and not taken to extremes. Your body will let you know when to stop.

It is also important to cool down after training. Cooling-down exercises tend to be more gentle than those for warming up. These will bring your body temperature back to normal, and relax your muscles and respiratory system.

Left: Always warm up thoroughly before starting your practice in order to avoid injuries.

Stretching

WRIST STRETCH

1. To stretch the tendons in the wrist, push the palms together firmly, pointing upward. Hold for 5 seconds, then repeat.
2. Press firmly, pointing the fingers outward. Hold for 5 seconds, then repeat.
3. Pointing the fingers downward, hold for 5 seconds, then repeat.

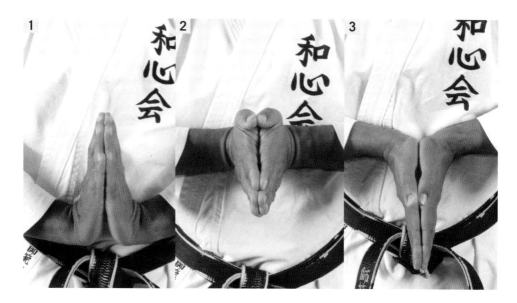

FIST AND FINGER STRETCH

1. Clench the fists as tightly as possible, hold for 5 seconds, then relax the hands.
2. Open the fists and stretch the fingers fully, then repeat, clenching the fists.

Repeat the entire drill for up to 30 seconds.

TRICEP STRETCH

Place the right arm under the outstretched left arm behind the elbow and pull firmly, stretching the tricep. Hold for 5–10 seconds before stretching the right tricep.

DELTOID STRETCH

Place the left hand between the shoulder blades and push down firmly on the left elbow with the right hand. Hold for 5–10 seconds before switching and stretching the right deltoid muscle.

HAMSTRING STRETCH

For a gentle hamstring stretch, place the right heel out, toes bent backward. Keep your hands clenched behind the back and, chin out, gently lean forward until the hamstring is pulled. Do not over-extend. Hold for 5–10 seconds before switching over and stretching the left hamstring.

GROIN STRETCH

Fully extend the left leg, and place the hands in front and gently lean forward, stretching the groin. Hold this position for 5–10 seconds before switching to the other leg and stretching in the same manner.

GROIN STRETCH WITH A PARTNER

It is essential that, when you have a partner assisting, you tell your partner when to stop— it is quite easy for an enthusiastic partner to overstretch you by putting too much force into the technique. Pull the soles of the feet together, and let your partner push your knees down gently, with you dictating how much pressure should be applied to the stretch. Hold the position for 10–15 seconds before releasing. Repeat the drill.

Sit with both legs fully extended. With your partner supporting your back, covering the spine as he or she pushes down, stretch the groin. Hold for 15 seconds before releasing.

Kihon waza
(basic techniques)

Punches

SEIKEN (BASIC PUNCH)

1. The fist is clenched firmly, with the thumb resting on top of the first and second fingers, compressing all the air out of the fist.
2. Side view of *seiken*.
3. *Tate seiken*. This shows *seiken* being delivered without the fist being twisted, with the thumb at the top of the fist. It can be used on virtually any target, and the striking area is the first two knuckles of the fist. Impact should always be made with those two knuckles.

JUNZUKI (LUNGE PUNCH)

This is used in most styles of karate, either as *junzuki* or *oizuki*. It is a front-hand lunge punch delivered in *zenkutsu dachi*—a long stance with the weight evenly distributed in the center, no wider than shoulder-width apart, with the front shin held at 90° and a straight back leg kept at an angle of 45°; the hips should also be at 45°.

GYAKUZUKI (REVERSE PUNCH)

This punch, like the *junzuki*, is used by all karate styles. With the left leg in front, the punch is delivered with the right fist at *chudan* level. The power is generated through speed of the technique as well as the body weight moving forward.

TOBIKOMIZUKI: HIDARI JODAN TSUKI (LEFT JODAN FACE PUNCH)

1. From *hidari shizentai dachi* (see stances, page 62), push the left leg forward, preparing to punch to the face with the front left fist.
2. Execute a left face punch (*jodan tsuki*) with the punching arm fully extended. Snap the fist back as soon as the punch is completed.

Strikes

URAKEN UCHI (BACK FIST)

1. As with the *seiken*, in the *uraken uchi*, the first two knuckles make impact.
2. Side view of *uraken uchi*.
3. As the attacker punches *gyakuzuki chudan* (to the body), the defender blocks with a left *teisho uchi* (palm heel block), and delivers a right *uraken uchi jodan* (to the face).

Although the striking area of *uraken uchi* is the face, it is often used for the stomach.

TETTSUI UCHI (BOTTOM FIST STRIKE)

The target areas are limitless with *tettsui uchi*, as the bottom of the fist has a soft area, which makes striking very easy.

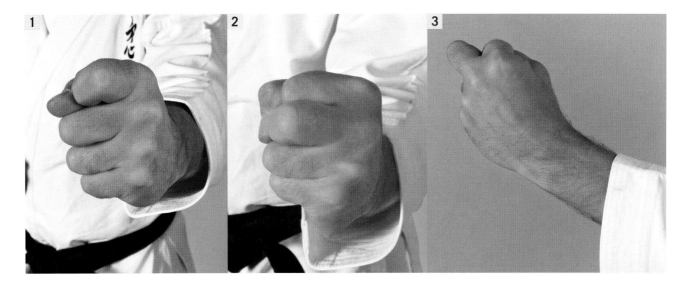

IPPON KEN UCHI (MIDDLE-KNUCKLE STRIKE, OR FIRST-FINGER STRIKE)

1. With *ippon ken uchi*, the target is usually the ribs or the face area, where penetration can be delivered with a very honed instrument, the knuckle.

2. *Nakadaka ippon ken* is delivered with the middle knuckle. The main striking areas are the ribs, where the knuckle penetrates the intercostals. These are the muscles that help to expand the rib cage. But again, it can be used for the face.

3. Side view of *nakadaka ippon ken*.

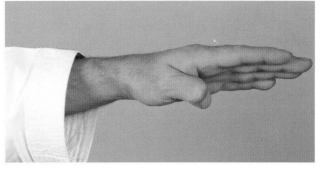

HAITO UCHI (RIDGE HAND)

The thumb should be tucked underneath and the hand tensed. This technique should be used primarily to the face, but it is a strong technique that can be used to the neck, stomach, or even groin.

NUKITE UCHI (FOUR-FINGER SPEAR HAND)

Target areas are limitless, but the *nukite uchi* is usually delivered straight to the face; the fingers strike the face and slide up to the eyes or nose.

SHUTO UCHI (KNIFE-HAND TECHNIQUE)

1. Target areas are limitless with the *shuto uchi*, as this strike is extremely strong no matter where it is applied. The hand is tensed and the thumb pulled back to strengthen the whole hand.
2. Another view of the *shuto uchi*.

IPPON NUKITE UCHI (ONE-FINGER SPEAR HAND)

Ippon nukite uchi is primarily used to attack the eyes.

TEISHO UCHI (PALM HEEL STRIKE)

1. *Teisho uchi* is a very powerful technique, pulling the fingers back using the palm of the hand. This is used to strike the solar plexus, or the groin when inverted.

2. As the attacker punches *gyakuzuki chudan* (to the body), the defender blocks with a left *gedan barai* and counters with a right *teisho uchi jodan* (to the face).

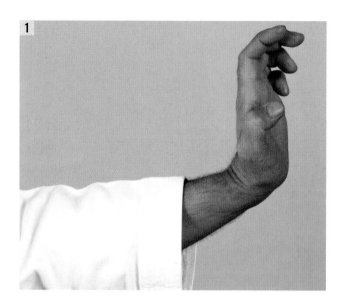

UDE UCHI (FOREARM STRIKE)

This is a forearm strike primarily used to attack the face or the ribs, and is a very powerful technique.

EMPI UCHI (ELBOW STRIKE)

1. This very powerful technique can be used at close range or while spinning, gaining maximum momentum, with the whole body weight behind the strike. It has limitless strike areas.

2. Side view of *empi uchi*.

3. *Empi uchi* being applied *jodan* (to the face).

Keri waza (kicking techniques)

SOKUTO FUMIKOMI (STAMPING, OR FOOT EDGE KICK)

1. Raise the right knee. The kick is either *sokuto* or *yoko-geri* (side stamping kick).
2. *Fumikomi* is the actual edge of the foot.
3. Applying *sokuto fumikomi* to the knee joint with the left foot.
4. *Sokuto fumikomi* is a powerful technique and can easily snap a leg if delivered correctly against the joint.

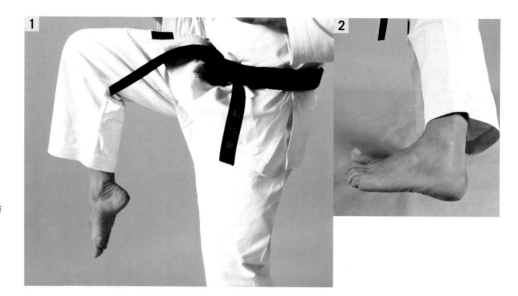

HIZA-GERI (KNEE STRIKE)

1. *Hiza-geri* is usually delivered to the groin, stomach, or even by pulling your opponent down and striking his face with your knee.

2. This shows *hiza-geri* being applied to an attacker's face. As the attacker grabs the opponent's collar, the opponent grabs his head and pulls him down onto her right knee.

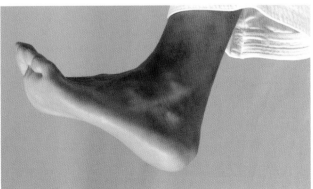

KAKATO-GERI (HEEL KICK)

Kakato-geri is used extensively with an axe kick. Its striking areas are limitless, but it is usually raised high to strike down either to the neck or the body.

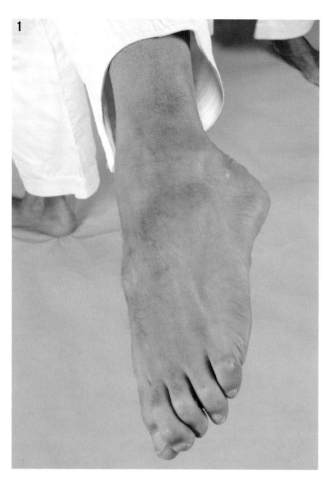
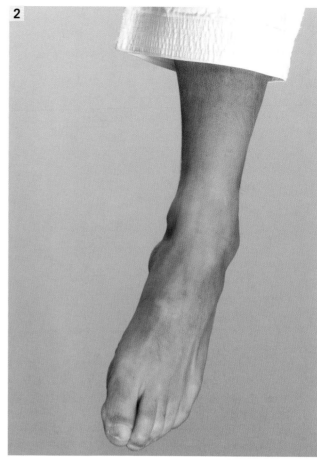

KIN-GERI (GROIN KICK)

1. The instep (*haisoku*) is used to kick the groin. *Haisoku* can also be the striking area for a roundhouse kick.

2. *Ashi kubi* (front of the foot) is used to kick the groin, body or head with a degree of control. When the ball of the foot or the heel are used, the technique is harder to control.

3. A *kin-geri* in action, kicking at groin-level height.

MAE-GERI
(FRONT SNAP KICK)

1. The right knee is raised, ready to deliver a front kick. Kicking with *koshi* (the ball of the right foot) and pushing the hip forward.
2. Raising the knee and extending the leg.
3. *Mae-geri* being snapped back.
4. *Mae-geri*, where the imaginary attacker is being pulled onto the kick.

USHIRO-GERI (BACK KICK)

1. Stand in *hidari hanmi gamae* (left fighting stance) facing the front.
2. The left leg is pulled across the body, twisting the body 180°, in preparation for turning and delivering a kick.
3. A *ushiro-geri chudan* (back kick) is delivered to the body using the heel. As the kick is completed, twist and drop down into the right stance.

USHIRO-MAWASHIGERI (SPINNING ROUNDHOUSE KICK)

1. Stand in *hidari hanmi gamae* (left fighting stance) facing the front.
2. The left leg is pulled across the body, twisting the body 180°, in preparation for turning and delivering a kick.
3. The *karate-ka* rotates, bringing the right leg up, spinning out, and delivering a spinning hook kick *chudan*.

TOBI NIDAN-GERI
(JUMPING DOUBLE FRONT KICK)

1. *Tobi nidan-geri* in left fighting stance.
2. The *karate-ka* jumps up and prepares the first kick at *chudan* level.
3. She then leaps and kicks with the left leg.
4. The second kick is delivered at *jodan* (head) height with the heel, landing in left stance.

TOBI YOKO-GERI
(JUMPING SIDE KICK)

A good example of a flying side kick. Designed primarily to knock assailants off their horses, this technique is now seen as ideal karate in its true form.

MAWASHI-GERI (ROUNDHOUSE KICK) AT *CHUDAN* LEVEL

1. Left fighting stance.
2. The *karate-ka* raises the right knee, preparing to kick.
3. She twists the right hip and extends the leg fully, striking with the right instep at *chudan* level.
4. The kick shown from a side angle.
5. *Mawashi-geri* being used against an opponent.

Stances

MUSUBI DACHI (READY STANCE)

Heels touching, toes spread at a 45° angle.

HEISOKU DACHI (FORMAL STANCE)

Big toes and heels touching.

NEKOASHI DACHI (CAT STANCE)

1. In this stance, 70 percent of the weight is on the back leg and 30 percent on the front leg, with the heel raised.
2. *Nekoashi dachi* performed by a Shotokan stylist.

GYAKU NEKOASHI DACHI (REVERSE CAT STANCE)

1. The reverse of the previous stance (*nekoashi dachi*), with 70 percent of weight on the front foot, 30 percent on the back foot, with the heel raised.
2. *Gyaku nekoashi dachi* shown from the side.

SANCHIN DACHI (HOURGLASS STANCE)

In *sanchin dachi*, the front foot is placed slightly in front of the back foot, usually the same length as the foot (i.e. 9–12 in/ 23–30 cm), and the feet are turned in.

Every style has variations of its length and width, but as a rule these stances go across all the four main schools: Shotokan, Wado-ryu, Shito-ryu, and Goju-ryu.

NAIHANCHI DACHI (HORSE-RIDING STANCE)

The feet are parallel or slightly turned in, and the knees pushed out. Again, different styles have slight variations, but this is generally termed *naihanchi dachi* or *tekki dachi*.

KIBA DACHI (STRADDLE STANCE)

This is the Shotokan stance, which has a very powerful posture. The feet are kept parallel, double the shoulder width, with the back kept straight.

KOKUTSU DACHI (BACK STANCE)

This is the Shotokan version of *kokutsu dachi*. The weight distribution is 70 percent to the back leg and 30 percent to the front. The hips are dropped low.

HIDARI SHIZENTAI DACHI (LEFT NATURAL STANCE)

This is used primarily in the practice of *tobikomizuki* and *nagashizuki* punching drills. The weight is evenly placed, but with either the left or right leg slightly in front. The body is kept relaxed and the arms held at the sides without tension.

SHIKODACHI (STRADDLE STANCE)

Knees and toes are pointing outward with the back kept straight. This stance is primarily used in *kata* training.

SAGIASHI DACHI (CRANE STANCE)

Standing on one leg, applying the technique. This stance is used primarily in *kata* training.

Blocks

JODAN UKE (FACE BLOCK)

The arm is at an angle above the head, with the other arm held close to the body.

MOROTE UKE (REINFORCED BLOCK)

The blocking arm is raised to approximately face height and the augmented block held just underneath it.

GEDAN BARAI (LOWER SWEEPING BLOCK)

1. The arm is held parallel to the thigh.
2. Side view of *gedan barai*.

HAISHO UKE (BACKHAND PALM, OR STRAIGHT BACKHAND BLOCK)

The whole forearm must be kept tense along with the back of the hand when applying this block.

Right: A right reverse punch to the body—*gyakuzuki chudan*.

UCHI UKE (INSIDE BLOCK)

Blocking in and down with the left forearm going completely past the body with the block. Shotokan stylists call this *soto uke*.

SOTO UKE (OUTSIDE BLOCK)

Blocking with the outside of the left forearm, rising from the right side of the body, *chudan* level, to *jodan* level of the left side of the body. Shotokan stylists call this block *uchi uke*.

Makiwara training

A *makiwara* is quite simply a padded striking board. Its origins are believed to be Chinese, but this has never been confirmed. It has been an extremely popular training tool in Japan ever since karate first arrived on the mainland in the 1920s, and remains so today.

Sizes of *makiwara* vary, as well as the padding, which used to be straw wrapped around a wooden post. Nowadays very stiff foam can be used, and this can be covered with rubber, canvas, or even leather.

Makiwara training is essential to correct punching techniques. It is especially good for developing the wrist of the punching arm. It is also important for hip strengthening for punches, strikes, and kicks, and it helps the grip strength for hands. Although not used as much these days due to the use of punch bags, I believe *makiwara* training is of huge benefit to the improvement of technique. The majority of dojo either have them mounted on the walls or use portable ones.

It is important that the body is kept relaxed when preparing to punch the *makiwara*. At the moment of impact, twist the fist, tense the abdomen, and feel the strength flow through the deltoid, shoulder, arm, and finally to the fist. It is essential that the *makiwara* is struck accurately and that, at the moment of contact, the hip is fully twisted. This action will enable the power of the body to be concentrated in the fist of the striking hand. Do not forget to expel the air sharply on the punch.

This principle of the execution of technique applies to striking and kicking of the *makiwara* board, not just to punching.

1. About to strike the *makiwara* pad with a right *seiken*.
2. Showing impact, where the back of the wrist is kept straight on impact.

Right: A traditional *makiwara* post from the early 1900s.

Right: The author demonstrating *tameshiwari* at the National Championships in England. An extremely high *mawashigeri jodan* (roundhouse kick) is used, using the ball of the foot (*koshi*).

Tameshiwari (spirit test)

EXERCISE 1

1. Preparing to break a wooden board using a *mawashi-geri* (roundhouse kick), at *jodan* height. The strike is made with the ball of the foot. The body weight must be behind the kick.
2. The break is made.

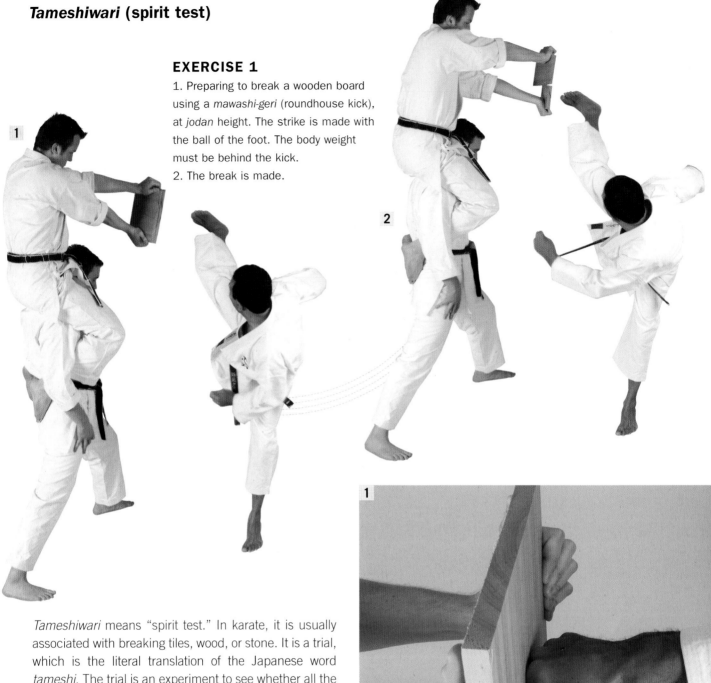

Tameshiwari means "spirit test." In karate, it is usually associated with breaking tiles, wood, or stone. It is a trial, which is the literal translation of the Japanese word *tameshi*. The trial is an experiment to see whether all the hard work of continuous repetitive training in karate-do has paid dividends. In the same way, *tameshigiri* ("trial by sword") is used in *kendo* ("way of the sword"), to test the strength of the blade—to find out whether the sword has a good weight and is flexible, especially during an actual cut.

Makiwara training is essential if *tameshiwari* is to be practiced. Once the student's limbs are strong enough and sufficient resistance strength has been built up in the body, *tameshiwari* can be practiced. A student must be of intermediate to advanced level before attempting to break items on a regular basis.

The technique is mainly a confidence booster for students and a way of demonstrating their powers with karate technique. It is not what true karate-do is about and does not reflect the ethos of the martial art; being able to break things is not the key accomplishment.

EXERCISE 2

1. Preparing to break a wooden board using *shuto uchi* (knife-hand strike) at *jodan* height. All the body weight must be behind the strike.

2. A successful break. The body moves quickly combined with a full hip twist as contact is made.

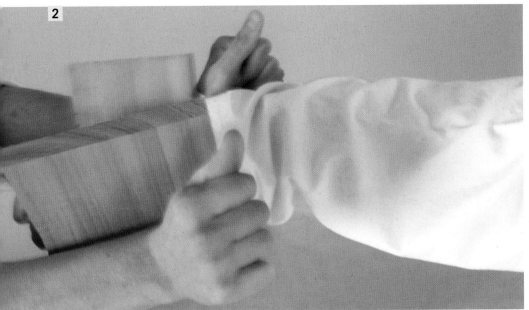

EXERCISE 3

1. Preparing to break a board with a right *seiken* punch, using the knuckles of the first and second fingers only.

2. Using a full hip twist, and the body weight behind the technique, a successful break is made.

The goal for all *karate-ka* is to be able to stop the opponent with one technique—*ikken hisatsu*, or to kill with one blow. A *karate-ka* will focus all his energy, both physically and mentally, into one technique, creating a focused energy, *kime*.

One of the ways of practicing this maneuver is on the *makiwara* board, then executing *tameshiwari*. It is not possible to actually use all the skills learned in karate on another human being, which is why inanimate objects are focused on in order to test the ability of a *karate-ka*.

Basic drills

Punches and blocks

These two punches and blocks are basic drills in the four major styles of karate-do.

1. Adopt *musubi dachi* (formal attention stance) and ready yourself.
2. Position yourself mentally and physically. "Yoi" (*hachiji dachi*).
3. Step forward into *hidari zenkutsu dachi* (left lunge punch stance).
4. Side view of *hidari dachi*.

5. Punch in *gyakuzuki dachi*—punching out with the right arm on the spot.
6. Lunge to the face with the weight distribution 55 percent on the front leg.
7. *Hidari gedan barai* (blocking stance).

Uchi waza (striking techniques)

STRIKING AREAS

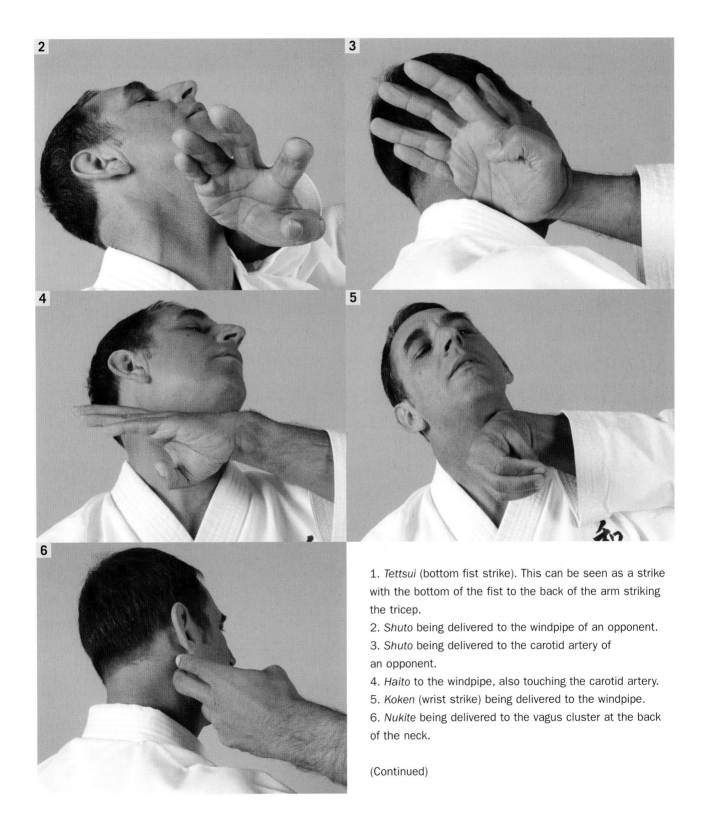

1. *Tettsui* (bottom fist strike). This can be seen as a strike with the bottom of the fist to the back of the arm striking the tricep.

2. *Shuto* being delivered to the windpipe of an opponent.

3. *Shuto* being delivered to the carotid artery of an opponent.

4. *Haito* to the windpipe, also touching the carotid artery.

5. *Koken* (wrist strike) being delivered to the windpipe.

6. *Nukite* being delivered to the vagus cluster at the back of the neck.

(Continued)

(Continued)

7. *Empi uchi* (elbow strike) being delivered to the back of the opponent's elbow.

8. *Empi* being delivered to the back of the opponent's elbow at head height.

9

9. *Empi* being delivered to the back of the opponent's head. Still a *jodan* strike, but the opponent has been pulled forward.

10. *Nukite* to the windpipe, pushing down into the windpipe, directly in front.

11. The same attack, from a slightly different angle. The hand is pushing into the throat.

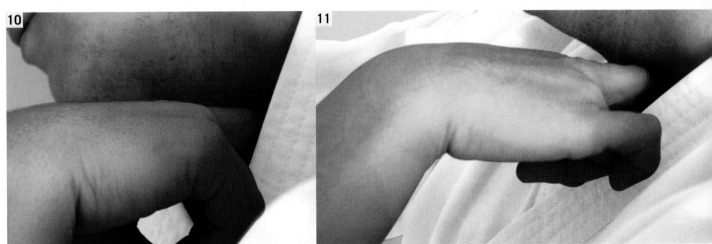

10

11

Nogare waza (escaping techniques)

EXERCISE 1

1. The opponent on the right grabs the defender around the throat.
2. The defender tries to push the opponent off.
3. The defender grabs the little fingers to force the opponent off.
4. A close-up of the little finger being grabbed.
5. The little finger is pulled back.
6. The defender finishes off the opponent with a *teisho* strike straight to the face.

EXERCISE 2

1. The attacker on the left is in *hidari hanmi gamae* (left fighting stance); the defender in *migi hanmi gamae* (right fighting stance).

2. The attacker lunges forward, punching to the defender's face with his left fist. The defender blocks *ude uke* (right forearm block), preventing the punch from striking his face.

3. The defender, with his right hand, strikes downward, hitting his opponent straight in the face.

Right: An *empi* strike with the right elbow.

Hente waza
(blocking and countering an
attack with the same limb)

This sequence of techniques is called *hente waza*. This is the technique of using the same limb both to block an attack and to counter by using a punch or strike.

In this next combination, the attacker is in *hidari hanmi gamae* (left fighting stance); the defender is in *migi hanmi gamae* (right fighting stance).

1. The attacker on the left steps forward and punches with his right fist to the body. The defender steps back and blocks *ude uke* with the left arm pointing downward, so he blocks in the middle of the forearm.

2. The defender continues pushing the arm out of the way, clearing the body adequately.

3. The defender immediately strikes with his left fist straight to the face. This shows the use of *hente waza*, using the same limb to block and defend.

4. The attacker is in the left stance; the defender in the right stance. The attacker reverse-punches on the spot with his right fist, punching *gyakuzuki chudan*.

5. With the attacker's arm fully extended, the defender withdraws, avoiding the punch.

6. The defender uses his right fist, striking *tettsui uchi* onto the attacker's outstretched arm, hitting the bicep/tricep area.

7. The defender immediately slides forward and strikes *empi* with his right elbow.

Ohyo gumite or yakusoku gumite (prearranged pairwork)

These are set prearranged pairs, which, if practiced regularly, become instinctive.

EXERCISE 1

1. The attacker is in the right stance; the defender in the left stance.
2. The attacker lunges to the face with the right fist; the defender blocks with the left arm, pushing the attacker's arm to the outside.
3. The defender delivers a *shuto* to the attacker's carotid artery with the right arm.
4. The defender immediately strikes *teisho* with the left palm to the attacker's stomach.
5. The defender pushes the attacker backward, making him take one complete step back.

6. The defender immediately counters with a right *mawashi-geri jodan*. The defender drops down to his left knee, watching the attacker's right leg.

7. As the attacker delivers a right *mawashi-geri* to the head, the defender pivots on his left knee, extending the right leg, preparing to sweep the attacker's supporting leg.

8. As the kick of the attacker is extended, the defender abruptly spins on his knee, aiming for the back of the attacker's knee on the supporting leg.

9. The defender spins around violently and strikes the back of the attacker's left leg.

10. The defender sweeps the attacker's supporting leg away from him.

(Continued)

(Continued)

11. The defender, still using the sweeping leg, raises it, preparing to kick the downed defender.

12. The defender strikes right *mawashi-geri chudan* or *jodan*, depending on where the attacker falls, while he is on his back.

13. The defender snaps his kicking leg back and starts to pivot around.

14. Both the attacker and defender pull away from each other.

15. The attacker and defender stand up, heels touching, and bow, thus completing the set pair technique.

EXERCISE 2

Quite often in set techniques, a student will instigate an attack and defeat his opponent. This is very realistic training.

1. The attacker on the right is in the left stance; the defender in the right stance.
2. The attacker kicks *mae-geri*; the defender takes one complete step back into the right stance.
3. The defender then lunges forward with his left leg, preparing to attack with a left *jodan tsuki*.
4. The defender lunges to the attacker's face. The attacker sidesteps and blocks *uchi uke*, striking the back of the defender's elbow.
5. The attacker grabs the defender's wrist, pushing the arm away.

(Continued)

(Continued)

6. The attacker prepares to strike with his right forearm to the defender's throat.

7. The attacker strikes *ude uchi*, straight to the defender's throat. At the same time, he turns the defender's wrist over, pressing his elbow against his chest.

8. The attacker puts all his weight against the defender's throat and, at the same time, pulls his arm, putting pressure on it.

9. The attacker bends his knees while keeping pressure on the defender's throat and arm.

10. The attacker leans back, dropping his weight as low as he possibly can, keeping his arms in position against the defender.

11. The attacker keeps dropping as low as his body will allow, making sure that the defender is made uncomfortable and is forced to come down with him.

12. The attacker falls backward onto his back, keeping the pressure on the defender's throat and arm.

13. The attacker falls back, releasing some of the pressure on the defender's throat and arm, which would otherwise result in severe damage.

14. The attacker raises his left leg, preparing to strike with *kakato*.

15. The attacker drops his left leg violently into the defender's groin.

16. The attacker releases the defender, and both prepare to roll out of the technique.

17. Both attacker and defender roll back onto their knees.

18. Both stand up and bow, ending the sequence.

EXERCISE 3

1. The attacker on the right is in the left stance; the defender is in the right stance.
2. The attacker punches and kicks simultaneously at the defender.
3. The defender sidesteps the attack, blocking the punch with his left, and *taisabbaki* (hip shifts) out of the way of the kick.
4. The defender instantly throws a left *furizuki* (swinging downward punch) to the attacker's sternum.

5. Following through, he punches with *shitazuki* (swinging upper punch) to the attacker's solar plexus.

6. He pulls both fists away, stepping back.

EXERCISE 4

1. The attacker throws *mawashi-geri jodan*; the defender leans back, avoiding the kick to the head.
2. The defender uses his left arm and knocks the *mawashi-geri* through, bringing his left arm behind him and pushing the kick away simultaneously, breaking the opponent's balance.
3. The defender immediately retaliates by raising his right knee, preparing to deliver *mawashi-geri jodan* back to his opponent's head.
4. The defender counters with *mawashi-geri jodan*.
5. As soon as the defender completes the kick, he quickly grabs the defender's collar with his right hand.

6. The defender sweeps the attacker's left leg away from him, simultaneously pulling on the back of the collar, as firmly as possible.

7. Pulling firmly and sweeping, he starts to pull down the attacker.

8. As the attacker falls, the defender does not let go of the collar; this way he controls where the attacker falls and keeps him within striking range.

9. As he pulls the attacker down, the defender also pulls him into him, preparing to counter.

10. The defender is poised, ready to punch the attacker's face.

11. The defender punches *jodantsuki*.

EXERCISE 5

1. The attacker on the left is in the right stance; the defender is in the left stance.

2. The attacker steps forward into the left stance, preparing to kick with his right leg.

3. As the attacker delivers a right *sokuto* (side kick), the defender steps forward at 45° diagonally, avoiding the kick and delivering *gedan barai*.

4. As the kick is extended, the defender immediately strikes *haito chudan*.

5. With the *haito chudan* against the opponent's stomach, the defender pushes the attacker in and at the same time pushes his hip directly underneath the attacker's hip.

6. The defender, using the opponent's momentum and his own inertia, pulls the attacker over his hip *nagi waza* (a throwing technique).

7. He drops the attacker directly to the floor.

8. Dropping the opponent straight onto his stomach and face, the defender immediately pins his attacker with the right knee.

9. The defender strikes *seiken* straight into the spine, immobilizing his opponent.

Kata training

Karate *kata* (formal exercises) was the only way karate was taught up until the 1930s. In the *kata*, all the elements of correct karate technique are stored. The vast majority of *kata* that are practiced in the dojo today and used on the tournament circuit can be traced right back to China or Okinawa. They appear to be dance-like drills, constantly repeated by students, yet hidden in these movements are hundreds of *kakushi waza* (secret techniques). These appear to be one form of technique, but in fact may be doing something completely different. Quite often, a technique that is performed while moving forward in *kata* practice is actually performed moving backward in a real combat situation.

Kata consists of many gymnastic movements, in which various offensive and defensive techniques are arranged harmoniously. The movements allow the student to

Above: Students practicing the stances that are required for *kata*.
Left: Teaching *kata* to a class of students and explaining what each move is used for makes the class interesting.

understand the relationship between the spirit and body, since *kata* are designed to develop them effectively.

Miyagi Chojun (1888–1953), founder of Goju-ryu karate and a leading master of modern karate, once said: "As a result of mind and body training, karate can build an indomitable spirit." It is this marriage of physical and mental strength that should be the goal of every karate student, and *kata* helps to achieve this.

One meaning of *kata* is "perfect form." There are many renowned karate pioneers who introduced *kata* to Japan, but the three karate men who are responsible for most of the *kata* that is taught and practiced today are:

- **Itosu, the teacher of Funakoshi (the founder of Shotokan)**
- **Higoanna (Higashionna), the teacher of Miyagi (Goju-ryu) and Mabuni (founder of Shito-ryu)**
- **Chojun Miyagi himself**

It is through these three pioneers that we continue to practice karate *kata*.

What is *kata*?

Kata was one person's way of memorizing certain fighting sequences *without* the use of a partner and to remember techniques that had a high rate of success when used in combat. Putting these movements into an organized drill that could be practiced regularly meant that they could not only be remembered more easily, but could also be taught to others. Many practitioners of Chinese martial arts, then Okinawan martial artists, continued this pattern.

What has now happened is that *kata* has become more than just an exercise in practicing karate. *Kata* has become a form of moving meditation that enhances both the mind and body. Learning to fight is not the ethos of karate-do; to karate traditionalists, learning to fight your failings is the true essence of the art, and this can be achieved through austere *kata* training.

While many *kata* techniques have been lost over the centuries, many remain, and it is through the *sensei* teaching them in the dojo that they are kept alive. They have also changed over the centuries. This is inevitable, as one *sensei* may add a technique and another may replace a technique. No matter, they are still a link to the past and to the creator of the *kata*. What is of interest is that as soon as a *kata* is performed, it is evident which style that practitioner studies. The four major styles each have a certain number of *kata* that they practice.

- Goju-ryu practice – 10 *kata*
- Wado-ryu practice – 10 *kata*
- Shotokan practice – 21 *kata*
- Shito-ryu practice – 43 *kata*

All the styles possess certain characteristics that can even identify the teacher as well as the style. I have listed the complete *kata* of each of the four major styles under the WKF list of *kata* allowed in competition (page 154).

Many modern styles of karate do not practice *kata* at all and, in my opinion, they are not really studying true karate-do. There is also no great merit in being able to remember lots of different *kata*. It is best to learn a few and understand them extremely well, rather than learn a lot and not know their true value. It takes many years to understand some *kata* fully. Many senior black belts often say it has taken more than 20 years for them to understand completely a *kata* they learned 15 years earlier.

Bunkai (the application of the *kata* techniques) is invaluable. Not all the *kata* can be deciphered, but many can, especially the more modern *kata*. It is this element, where the *kata* can be broken down and the techniques put into practice, that allows the student to really "know" the *kata* and to polish and "buff it up" constantly until the moves become refined. A perfect display of *kata* is where seeing the practitioner perform the *kata* enables you to visualize an actual fight taking place without an opponent. The true essence of karate-do is in the continuous practice of *kata*.

Kata is also performed in competition and has produced world champions in WKF tournaments. These contests had their origins in Japanese universities, as well as the larger Japanese organizations. One of the major concerns for many senior *sensei* is karate competition tournaments geared only for children. It takes many years of practice to fully understand and know *kata*; however, many juniors in age, who have learned the moves to many *kata*—including some very technically difficult ones—are still under the age of 12.

I believe that introducing karate to children is a positive move. The earlier they are introduced to the discipline of karate-do, the more beneficial it will be to them, especially in later life. If their *sensei* teaches them not only the physical aspects of karate, but also the ethos of the art, especially through *kata* training, then he or she will have provided an invaluable service.

Competition *kata* is a a different matter, however. I do not believe that the majority of karate *sensei* around the world force their very young students to compete in *kata* competition on a regular basis, but unfortunately many do. The *sensei* may be encouraged and even persuaded to enter the child into competition by the parents, for many reasons. Does the child really understand what they are doing? Do they know what the moves represent? I believe that the child understands only the aesthetic movements. It could also be kudos for the *sensei* to boast he has many *kata* champions in the dojo. I am not against competitions held solely for children, but I am, like other *sensei*, concerned that extremely difficult *kata* are being taught to very young children who cannot possibly understand what they are learning. Karate is a martial art, and I often think instructors forget this. The techniques practiced in *kata* are there to maim and even kill, but I doubt very much if this is being conveyed to the student when they are being taught the moves.

competitions, and I hope it does not lead to *kata* being seen as purely a dance routine, which is a reputation it has already gained with many *karate-ka* who have never been taught correctly.

Today, it is through the judging of *kata* that an effect is being felt on how the *kata* are being taught in the dojo. Instructors who are also karate officials are looking at the aesthetic appearance of *kata*, rather than the martial aspect. This is a cause for concern, as it will erode the *kata* movements from their original form and thus negate the true meaning of the technique. Tournament officials will have to prevent this situation from occurring by getting to know all *kata* that are being performed in competition, or making sure that the majority of officials on the *tatami* (mat) know the *kata*. This way the true *kata* will not be lost, as many have been in the past.

The issue of competition aside, however, *kata* is mandatory in karate gradings, and a high level of performance must be given if a pass is to be acquired. The *kata* demonstrated in this book is performed by Yoshinobu Ohta, the JKA Shotokan Chief Instructor for England.

I suspect that one of the reasons karate has still not been accepted by the IOC as an Olympic sport is because of this anomaly. Some karate organizations will not allow their students to compete in either *kata* or *kumite* competition until they reach the age of 16. Their reason for this is simple: the student has not reached a level of maturity where they can interpret controlled anger. Many can, but usually they are over the age of 16. We shall see what the future holds for junior karate

Jion kata (temple ground)

The origin of *jion kata* is unknown. It probably came from China, as did many of the *kata* we now practice, and is often linked with two other *kata*, *jiin* and *jitte*, both of which are much shorter than *jion*. Anko Itosu (1830–1915) must be credited for the versions practiced nowadays by most karate schools. Itosu is known to have practiced *jion* on a regular basis, and taught it to his students.

Jion translates as "temple ground," and one theory is that it was taught by monks. Although this cannot be proven, it is widely accepted by many *karate-ka* in both Okinawa and Japan.

The version of *jion kata* shown here is that of the Japanese Karate Association Shotokan.

1. *Yoi* ready position.
2. Step back with the left leg preparing to block.
3. Perform right *chudan uchi uke* and left *gedan uke* in right *zenkutsu dachi*.
4. Step forward with the left leg, preparing to block.

5. Perform *ryoken chudan kakiwake uke* in left *zenkutsu dachi*.
6. Kick right *chudan mae-geri*.
7. Punch right *chudan tsuki* in right *zenkutsu dachi*.
8. Punch left *chudan tsuki*.

9. Punch right *chudan tsuki*.

10. Slide in, then out with the left leg, preparing to block.

11. Perform *ryoken chudan kakiwake uke* in right *zenkutsu dachi*.

12. Kick left *chudan mae-geri*.

13. Punch left *chudan tsuki* in left *zenkutsu dachi*.

(Continued)

(Continued)

14. Punch right *chudan tsuki*.
15. Punch left *chudan tsuki*.
16. Slide left leg to the left, preparing to block.
17. Perform left *jodan age uke* in left *zenkutsu dachi*.
18. Punch right *chudan gyakuzuki*.

19. Slide right leg forward, preparing to block.
20. Perform right *jodan age uke* in right *zenkutsu dachi*.
21. Punch left *chudan gyakuzuki*.
22. Slide left leg forward, preparing to block.
23. Perform left *jodan age uke* in left *zenkutsu dachi*.

24. Step forward and punch right *chudan junzuki* in right *zenkutsu dachi*, and *kiai*.

25. Pivot 180°, preparing to block.

26. Perform right *jodan uchi uke* and left *gedan uke* with right *kokutsu dachi*.

27. Prepare to punch.

28. Perform right *kagizuki*, left *yoriashi kiba dachi*.

29. Prepare to block on the right side.

(Continued)

(Continued)

30. Perform left *jodan uchi uke* and right *gedan uke* in left *kokutsu dachi*.

31. Prepare to punch.

32. Perform left *kagizuki*, right *yoriashi kiba dachi*.

33. Step forward with the left leg and perform left *gedan barai* in left *zenkutsu dachi*.

34. Step forward, preparing to strike.

35. Perform right *teisho*, *chudan*, *yoko uchi kibadachi*.

36. Step forward, preparing to strike.

37. Perform left *teisho*, *chudan*, *yoko uchi kibadachi*.

38. Step forward, preparing to strike.

39. Perform right *teisho*, *chudan*, *yoko uchi kibadachi*.

40. Pivot 180°, preparing to block.

41. Perform right *jodan uchi uke*, left *gedan barai* in right *kokutsu dachi*.

42. Prepare to block.

43. Pull the right leg to the left and perform left *jodan morote uke—heisoku dachi*.

44. Prepare to block.

45. Step out with the right leg and perform left *jodan uchi uke*, right *gedan barai*, left *kokutsu dachi*.

(Continued)

(Continued)

46. Prepare to block.

47. Pull the left leg to the right and perform left *jodan morote uke—heisoku dachi*.

48. Cross the arms and perform *ryoken gedan kakiwake* in *heisoku dachi*.

49. As above, seen from the reverse angle.

50. Raise the right leg, preparing to block.

51. Perform *gedan kosauke*, right front *kosa dachi*.

52. Step back with the left leg and perform *ryoken gedan kakiwake* in right *zenkutsu dachi*.

53. Step forward with the left leg, preparing to block.

54. Perform *ryoken chudan kakiwake* in left *zenkutsu dachi*.

55. Step forward with the right leg, preparing to block.

56. Perform *ryoken jodan kosauke* in right *zenkutsu dachi*.

57. Perform right *jodan uraken uchi* in right *zenkutsu dachi*.

58. Perform left *chudan tsuki uke*, right above-shoulder *kamae*.

59. Perform right *jodan uraken uchi*, left *zenwan munemae kamae*.

60. Pivot 270°, preparing to block.

61. Perform left *chudan uchi uke*, left *zenkutsu dachi*.

(Continued)

(Continued)

62. Step forward with the right leg, preparing to punch.

63. Right *chudan junzuki*, right *zenkutsu dachi*.

64. Pull the right leg back, preparing to turn 180°.

65. Perform right *chudan uchi uke*, right *zenkutsu dachi*.

66. Step forward with the left leg, preparing to punch.

67. Perform left *chudan junzuki*, left *zenkutsu dachi*.

68. Retract the left leg, preparing to block 90° to your left.

69. As above, seen from the reverse angle.

70. Perform left *gedan barai*, left *zenkutsu dachi*.

71. Raise the right leg and right arm, preparing to strike.

72. Perform right *zenwan chudan otoshi*, right *fumikomi kiba dachi*.

73. Raise the left leg and left arm, preparing to strike.

74. Perform left *zenwan chudan otoshi*, left *fumikomi kiba dachi*.

75. Raise the right leg and right arm, preparing to strike.

76. Perform right *zenwan chudan otoshi*, right *fumikomi kiba dachi*.

(Continued)

(Continued)

77. Retract the left leg, preparing to grab.

78. As above, seen from the reverse angle.

79. Perform left *chudan sokumenzuki*, with the right fist in front of the right nipple, and left *yoriashi kiba dachi*.

80. Cross the body with the left arm, preparing to grab.

81. Perform right *chudan sokumenzuki*, with the left fist in front of the left nipple, and right *yoriashi kiba dachi* and *kiai*.

82. (Right) The last position in *kata* is the same as the first.

Nage waza (throwing techniques)

Throwing techniques are quite common in karate-do. They may not be part of a grading syllabus, but are often taught to a student to show that there is a lot more to karate-do than just kicking and punching. Many senior *sensei* will teach all aspects of karate-do, including *shimi waza* (choking techniques) and *osaekomi waza* (immobilization techniques), as well as many *nage waza* (throwing techniques).

Most of the early Okinawan karate pioneers who settled in Japan during the early twentieth century had a vast knowledge of all aspects of martial arts. These skills were passed on to the students along with their karate training.

The Dai Nippon Butokukai (the Japanese government-recognized controlling body for all martial arts) would only recognize karate as a true martial art if it were seen to be a complete fighting system. It was accepted into the organization because karate practitioners could not only punch, strike, and kick, but also used *nogare* (escaping techniques) from locks placed on them. They showed the use of *kawashi* (avoiding), as well as *taisabaki* (hip and body evasion), *nagashi* (sweeping away), *irimi* (entering an attack), and, lastly, *nage waza* (throwing techniques). All these elements combined with *tsuki* (punching), *uchi* (striking), *keri* (kicking), and *uke* (blocking), made karate an acceptable and completely new martial art.

Left: An attack is countered, and the defender steps behind the assailant and quickly throws him, completely disorientating him.

Ji yu kumite (freestyle sparring)

Ji yu kumite practice (freestyle sparring) is the ultimate test of any *karate-ka*'s skills. Attacking, blocking, and countering with all the techniques that the student has been taught are a test not just of physical prowess, but also the mental attitude toward others. It is a test of endurance and spirit. In *ji yu kumite*, the student is trying to make controlled contact using as many different techniques as possible. This is very challenging, and extremely rewarding when successful. The targets are limited and so are the permitted techniques. There is, however, still a vast repertoire of techniques to draw upon.

Some techniques in *ji yu kumite* are difficult to execute with control. These must be practiced regularly and diligently, until the student has mastered them and can include them in his or her repertoire. A good attitude must always be predominant in *ji yu kumite*. Without it, severe injury can easily be caused. The Japanese word for a good fighting spirit is *toh-kon*. *Kakato-geri* (axe kick) and *ushiro mawashi-geri* (back spinning kick) are two such difficult techniques, and when used correctly they are very spectacular. *Ashi barai* (leg sweeping) is also encouraged in *ji yu kumite*, as it is in judo, and many advanced sweeps with a follow-up technique such as a punch or kick are now seen in karate tournaments.

Techniques not allowed in *ji yu kumite* are those that could maim or even kill. In addition, open-hand technique is not encouraged near the face, as this could lead to loss of sight (e.g. *nukite*/spear hand, with one, two, or four fingers). *Kansetsu-geri* (joint kicks) are not allowed, and nowadays *kingeri* (groin kick) is discouraged. Some schools of karate still allow *kingeri* to be used in *ji yu kumite*; however, groin guards are expected to be worn.

The earlier a *sensei* gets the student to start practicing

Above left: Students in Hong Kong being shown striking areas that can be used in a fight situation and that will also score points in competition.

Above right: Students practicing the techniques taught in *ji yu kumite* routines.

ji yu kumite, the better. Initially, it is best to start with a senior grade, who will allow the student to progress slowly. This way the student is allowed to practice attacks and blocks, and can be corrected where necessary.

In *ji yu kumite*, it is best to put combination attacks together, rather than try to hit the opponent with a single technique. This is an obvious approach to take, as if an attack is made with a single blow or the technique is blocked, a counterattack could follow.

With higher grades, the chances of any self-inflicted injury are greatly reduced. The vast majority of injuries that do occur when practicing *ji yu kumite* are to the fingers and toes. This is due to several factors: the fist is not correctly clenched when punching; the toes are not correctly pulled back on front kicks; or pulled down sufficiently on roundhouse kicks. It takes time to correct these minor obstacles, and the only way to improve is with constant practice.

Ji yu kumite can be enjoyed in the same way as basic *kihon* and *kata* practice if taught correctly. A hatred or phobia of it can quickly occur, however, if an unpleasant incident happens. This is why it is essential that all classes with lower grades are supervised by the *sensei*.

Practicing *ji yu kumite*

Above: Delivering a right knife hand to the throat of an attacker (*migi shutouchi jodan*).

In the practice of *ji yu kumite*, *karate-ka* should stay relaxed and ready to react to their opponent's every move. *Karate-ka* should be prepared to attack at every opportunity with the wide variety of techniques that they have built into their arsenal, as well as using blocking and countering moves.

Some *karate-ka* prefer to dance around the dojo in a Muhammad Ali style, while others remain quite static and statuesque in composure. Regularly changing stance from left to right, and vice versa, is important. This will prevent the opponent from creating an attack and disrupting their pattern. Moving around the dojo and changing the angle at which the opponent is faced will have the same effect.

Whatever style of fighting method is adopted, attacks and counterattacks are fast and furious, and over in a blinding flash. It is important to remain calm during fighting training, especially in the early stages of practice. Once the adrenaline rush has passed, the body will move more smoothly, with the technique flowing rather than jerky.

Injury is uncommon in *ji yu kumite* training, especially with higher graded students, due to superb control of the technique (*sun dome*—control within an inch, especially to the face). If a *karate-ka* is swept over, he or she will quickly bounce up and continue with practice. The movements of the *karate-ka* are instinctive, not rehearsed, and several maneuvers can be executed in literally seconds.

Above all, *ji yu kumite* is fun and exhilarating, as well as challenging. A feeling of satisfaction is always felt at the end of practice, no matter how successful or unsuccessful the *karate-ka* has been with his or her performance.

Ji yu kumite sequences

EXERCISE 1

1. The two *karate-ka* stand opposite each other in *"yoi"* (*hachiji dachi*—position ready) to commence their *ji yu kumite* practice.

2. Both adopt left fighting stance (*hidari hanmi gamae*).

3. The fighter on the right throws a right *haito* (ridge hand) to the face. The fighter on the left blocks the attack with his right palm.

4. The fighter on the left immediately punches *gyakuzuki chudan* (reverse punch) with his left fist. The fighter on the right blocks the *gyakuzuki* using a left *teisho uke* (palm heel strike).

5. The fighter on the right counterpunches with a left *gyakuzuki chudan*, hitting his opponent in the body.

EXERCISE 2

1. The fighter on the left throws a *jodan tsuki* (face punch) with his right fist. The fighter on the right blocks, using a *jodan uke* (face block).

2. The fighter on the right counters with a *migi mawashi-geri jodan* (right roundhouse kick to the head). The fighter on the left blocks the kick with a right *ude uke* (forearm block).

EXERCISE 3

1. The fighter on the right throws a right *shuto* (knifehand strike) to the face.

2. He immediately throws a left *gyakuzuki jodan* (reverse punch to the head).

3. Without any pause, the fighter on the right attacks with a *ura mawashi-geri jodan* (hook kick to the head) with his right heel, hitting his opponent across the face.

EXERCISE 4

1. The fighter on the left executes a right *ura mawashi-geri jodan* (hook kick to the head). The fighter on the left drops down to avoid the kick.

2. As the fighter on the right rises up, the fighter on the left immediately snaps his right leg back to attack with a right *mawashi-geri jodan* (roundhouse kick to the face). This is blocked by the fighter on the right using a *shuto* with his right hand.

3. As the fighter on the left drops his kicking leg, the fighter on the right sweeps the fighter's right leg with a *hidari ashi barai* (left foot sweep) using the sole of his foot.

4. The fighter on the right follows up, as the fighter on the left drops down, with a right *gyakuzuki chudan* (reverse punch to the body).

EXERCISE 5

1. The fighter on the right feints as if he is going to throw a right *jodan tsuki* (strike to the face). The fighter on the left pulls back ready to block.

2. The fighter on the right raises his right knee and kicks a *mae-geri chudan* (front kick to the body) using the ball of his right foot. The fighter on the left blocks the kick using a *gedan barai* (left arm) lower sweep.

3. The fighter on the left grasps the kicking leg of the fighter on the right with his left arm and, at the same time, grabs the jacket with his right hand. Without hesitation, he sweeps the attacker's supporting leg away using a right *ashi barai* (foot sweep).

4. The fighter on the left finishes off the attacker, whom he has dropped on the ground, with a right *gyakuzuki chudan* (reverse punch to the body).

EXERCISE 6

1. Both fighters face each other in *migi dachi* (right stance).
2. The fighter on the right raises his right knee and throws a *yoko-geri* (side kick) at the fighter on the left. The fighter on the left pulls his body back to avoid the kick.

3. The fighter on the left retaliates by raising his right knee and countering with a right *yoko-geri jodan* (side kick to the head). The fighter on the right leans back to avoid the kick.

EXERCISE 7

1. The fighters face each other and bow (*rei*).
2. The fighter on the left attacks with a combination of *waza* techniques. Her first attack is a *mawashi-geri jodan* (roundhouse kick to the head) with her left leg. The defender leans back to avoid the attack.

3. She follows it immediately with a *gyakuzuki chudan* (reverse punch to the body) with her right fist. Again, the defender leans away from the onslaught.
4. She finally hits her opponent with a *yoko-geri chudan* (side kick to the body).

EXERCISE 8

1. The fighters face each other and bow (*rei*).
2. The fighter on the left comes out fast and punches her partner with a *gyakuzuki chudan* (reverse punch to the body).
3. Without any hesitation, she follows up with a right *uramawashigeri jodan* (hook kick to the head), forcing the defender to step back to avoid the kick.

EXERCISE 9

1. The attacker on the left throws a left *mawashi-geri jodan* (roundhouse kick to the head). She forces the defender around by adjusting her position.
2. She then throws a right *gyakuzuki chudan* (reverse punch), hitting the fighter on the left.
3. Even though contact was made with the punch, she transfers the weight onto her left leg and throws a right *mawashi-geri jodan* (roundhouse kick to the head), just missing her opponent's face.

Karate *waza* used in defense

At intermediate to advanced level, most *karate-ka* have a decent knowledge of how to use their technique in a self-defense situation without maiming or killing their attackers. An example is shown here using a technique that is often seen in *kata* practice, but not often understood as to its application. The technique is called *mawashi uke*.

1. The aggressor (on the left) makes a move to attack the throat of his victim.

2. The defender prepares to stop the attack and bring his left hand over to strike his attacker's left hand, and his right hand over ready to strike his attacker's right hand.

3. Before the attacker can get a firm grip around the throat, the defender strikes both arms of the attacker on the lower forearm.

4. The defender quickly begins to wrap the attacker's arms

across each other while the attacker's body momentum is still coming forward.

5. The defender still moves both his arms clockwise, beginning to lock up the attacker.

6. The defender at great speed continues the circle, moving his arm through 180°.

7. The attacker is immobilized, with his arms completely locked up.

8. The defender continues to complete the lock, taking his

arms through 270° (this maneuver is often seen in *kata* as a fast circular motion).

9. The defender then compresses the attacker's arms and body by moving forward and putting severe pressure on the attacker's arms.

10. The attacker is completely locked up and unable to move as the defender wraps his arms around the attacker's back.

11. The attacker is then struck in the groin by the defender's left knee.

Competition karate

As mentioned previously, the World Karate Federation (WKF) is the only controlling body of karate recognized by the International Olympic Committee (IOC). Since the early 1950s, the need for a controlling body for karate had been felt, as the popularity of karate was becoming a phenomenon. It was in 1960 that an international body was formed, and named the World Union of Karate Organizations (WUKO). In June 1985, WUKO was officially recognized by the IOC. Over the following years, WUKO's membership increased dramatically, and the majority of its membership was recognized by the IOC.

Fédération Mondiale de Karate (World Karate Federation) was the name given to WUKO in 1993. This body was formed in Algeria, and since then has increased its membership to more than 170 member countries and millions of students throughout the world.

Left: Two women competing in a karate *shiai* competition. One wears a red belt (*aka*) and one wears a blue belt (*ao*).
Below: Performing a *gyakuzuki chudan*.

Karate-ka attire

All competitors must wear white, unmarked karate suits (*do-gi*). No headbands or jewelry are permitted, and competitors must have short fingernails. Protective groin boxes are allowed, but the wearing of glasses is not. Soft contact lenses may be worn instead.

Women are allowed to wear a plain white t-shirt under their karate jackets, as well as protective breast padding for *kumite*. A discreet hair clip is permitted in *kata*.

Competition *kumite*

Categories

There are four categories for WKF *kumite* competition.

These are then divided into male, female, cadet, and junior events. In *kumite* events, they are then divided into weight categories. The four categories are:

- Individual *kata*
- Team *kata*
- Individual *kumite*
- Team *kumite*

Team *kata* has either three male or three female competitions performing *kata* in unison.

Below: Three female competitors who have been medalists in English National competitions on many occasions.

There are both male and female teams in team *kumite*. The male teams consist of seven members, five of which may compete in a round. The female team comprises five members, with three of these allowed to compete in a round.

WKF competition rules

This style of karate competition is deemed as semi-contact (see page 129). Competition bouts take place on a flat matted surface, which must be 26 ft sq (8 meters sq). Most combat areas are matted (*tatami*) in one color for the main fighting area. The border around the fighting area is usually in another color to indicate the *jogai* (area outside the fighting area).

There are four officials around the *tatami* area: the judges and the referee. An arbitrator, timekeeper, and recordkeeper are also present at the fighting area. *Kumite* bouts are three minutes each for men and two minutes for women, cadets, and juniors.

Individual *kumite* bouts are between *aka* (red belt), who stands on the referee's right side and *ao* (blue belt), who stands on the left of the referee. The competitors face each other at a distance of 10 ft (3 meters), and the referee will start the bout with the command "*shobu hajime.*" The moment a score is made or there is an infringement of the rules, the referee will shout "*yame*" to stop the bout. Once the competitors have returned to their starting lines, a score will be given (*aka* or *ao-no kachi*), or a penalty, or warning of a penalty if an infringement of the rules occurred. If one competitor gains an advantage of eight points over his rival, the bout will be stopped and that competitor will be declared the winner. Otherwise, the bout will last for its full duration, then a decision on the outcome of the bout will be made.

As explained under WKF rules for karate competition (see page 34), the competitors are encouraged to use as many different techniques to score with as possible. This can make for an exciting competition and is reflected in the scores given, even though attacks are limited to certain areas of the body. The target areas for attack are: head, face, neck, abdomen, chest, back, and side of the body.

A competitor will be awarded an *ippon* (one point) for:
- *Chudan* or *jodan tsuki* (middle-level or face punch)
- *Chudan* or *jodan uchi* (middle-level or face strike)

A competitor will be awarded a *nihon* (two-point) score for:
- *Chudan* (middle-level) kick
- Punches on the back, including back of the head and neck
- Combination hand techniques, the individual components of which each score in their own right
- Unbalancing the opponent and scoring

A competitor will be awarded *sanbon* (three points) for:
- *Jodan* kicks
- Throwing or leg-sweeping the opponent to the mat, followed by a scoring technique

A score will be given only if it meets the following criteria:
- Good form
- Sporting attitude
- Vigorous application
- Awareness (*zanshin*)
- Good timing
- Correct distance

It is essential that competitors stay alert at all times throughout a bout. *Zanshin* (awareness) should be present at all times, otherwise serious injury may occur.

Right: Performing *mawashi-geri jodan* in competition.

Prohibited behavior

Elements that will cause injury and by their very nature are dangerous are prohibited from use in *kumite* matches. Penalties are issued to the competitors if they carry out any of the following:

CATEGORY I OFFENSES

- Techniques that make excessive contact, having regard to the scoring area attacked, and techniques that make contact to the throat.
- Attacks to the arms, legs, groin, joints, or instep.
- Attacks to the face with open-hand techniques.
- Dangerous or forbidden throwing techniques.

CATEGORY II OFFENSES

- Feigning or exaggerating injury.
- Repeated exits from the competition area (*jogai*).
- Self-endangerment by indulging in behavior that exposes the contestant to injury by the opponent, or failing to take adequate measures for self-protection (*mubobi*).
- Avoiding combat as a means of preventing the opponent from scoring.
- Clinching, wrestling, pushing, seizing without attempting to throw, or other technique.
- Techniques that by their nature cannot be controlled for the safety of the opponent, and dangerous and uncontrolled attacks.
- Attacks with the head, knees, or elbows.
- Talking to or goading the opponent, failing to obey the orders of the referee, discourteous behavior toward the refereeing officials or other breaches of etiquette.

SHINGI

Instructors can often find that students have wonderful technique, with good form and balance, but as soon as they compete in *kumite* they lose. It is quite often put down to *shingi*—where the martial awareness is not in tune with the physical prowess. It is not enough simply to learn the physical techniques of karate. Mental development must also be part of the training. It is important to watch the opponent's every action and tune into every signal that is being put out. This process of learning is called *shingi*, and maintaining both physical and mental awareness at all times is key.

PENALTIES

The following penalties will be given for infringement of any of the rules of *kumite* competition.

***Chukoku* (warning):** This may be imposed for minor infractions or the first instance of a minor infraction.

***Keikoku*:** *Ippon* (one point) is added to the opponent's score in this penalty. *Keikoku* is imposed for minor infractions after a warning has previously been given in the bout, or for infractions not sufficiently serious to merit *hansoku-chui*.

***Hansoku-chui*:** *Nihon* (two points) is added to the other opponent's score in this penalty. *Hansoku-chui* is usually imposed for infractions for which a *keikoku* has previously been given in the bout, although it may be imposed directly for serious infringements that do not meet *hansoku*.

***Hansoku*:** This is imposed following a very serious infraction, or when a *hansoku-chui* has already been given. It results in the disqualification of the contestant who has committed the *hansoku* offence. In team matches, the fouled competitor's score will be set at eight points, and the offender's score will be zeroed.

***Shikkaku*:** This is a disqualification from the actual tournament, competition, or match. In order to define the limit of *shikkaku*, the Referee Council must be consulted.

Shikkaku may be invoked when a contestant:

- Fails to obey the orders of the referee
- Acts maliciously
- Commits an act that harms the prestige and honor of karate-do
- Is considered to violate the rules and spirit of the tournament by their actions

In team matches, the fouled competitor's score will be set at eight points and the offender's score will be zeroed.

A result is determined by the competitor who has accrued the most points at the end of a bout. If there is no winner after the allotted time of the bout, any decisions against a competitor will be taken into account. If there is still a draw, then *encho-sen* (extension of the bout) may be called by the referee. If this is not possible,

Left: A well-positioned *gyakuzuki chudan* punch, like this one, will earn the competitor an *ippon* (one point score).

semi-contact karate tournaments. Kicks and punches are allowed to the body, as well as certain sweeping (unbalancing) techniques. Kicks and strikes to the groin are disallowed, as well as punching to the chest in women's *kumite*.

Full-contact: This form of competition still has its restrictions. Strikes to the head, neck, or back using either hand or elbow strikes are not allowed. Kicks or strikes to the groin or breasts are also disallowed. Elbow strikes to the body, along with punches, are allowed, however, as well as kicks to the head, body, and legs. Knee kicks are allowed after grabbing the opponent, and throwing techniques can be executed as long as the hold is released after a throw.

Jissen training (actual fighting)

Some karate groups allow *jissen* training in the dojo. *Jissen* is actual combat where every and any technique is allowed. It is an extremely dangerous exercise, and is not encouraged by the majority of organizations; however, *karate-ka* who participate in cage fighting, where different martial artists compete against each other for large sums of money, say it is invaluable training. It now attracts a lot more students who have either been training for full-contact competitions or kickboxing tournaments.

Many karate *sensei* will still not permit *jissen* practice in their dojo.

a decision will be made by the whole referee panel, and will be based on the following criteria:

- **Fighting spirit**
- **Good attitude**
- **Strength**
- **Tactics**
- **Technique**
- **Contestant initiative in the majority of the actions**

Karate tournaments

In karate tournaments, there are three types of competition.

Non-contact: In many styles of karate, it is believed that a competitor's practice of karate technique is too dangerous, and therefore no contact is allowed. A form of competition is practiced; however, no contact with the face or body is permitted.

Semi-contact: The rules of Shobu Ippon (one-point fighting) as well as the WKF rules come under this heading. Certain techniques are still not allowed in

CAGE FIGHTING

Cage fighting is a new form of exhibition fighting that has become very popular this century. It is combat against all and every form of martial artist or even pugilist, where prize money is the reward. It attracts many *karate-ka* and spectators in the same way that crowds gathered to watch gladiators of ancient times fight to the death. The rules are very simple: no eye gouging or stamping on the hand. Other than that, everything else is allowed.

Referees' commands and signals for WKF *kumite* competition

1. *Shobu hajime* (start the match). After the announcement is given by the referee, he takes one step back.

2. *Ippon* (one point). The referee extends his arm downward at a 45° angle on the side of the person who has scored.

3. *Nihon* (two points). The referee extends his arm at shoulder level on the side of the scorer.

4. *Sanbon* (three points). The referee extends his arm upward at a 45° angle on the side of the person who has scored.

5. *Shomen-ni-rei* (bow to the front). The referee extends his arms palms to the front.

6. *Otagai-ni-rei* (bow to each other). The referee motions to the contestants to bow to each other.

7. *Yame* (stop). Interruption, end of the match, or bout. As he makes the announcement, the referee makes a downward chopping motion with his hand.

8. *Yame* shown from the side.

9. *No kachi* (winner). Given at the end of the match or bout, announcing *aka* or *ao-no kachi*. The referee extends his arm upward at a 45° angle on the side of the winner.

10. Referee's opinion. After calling "*yame*" and using the prescribed signal, the referee indicates his preference by holding his bent arm palm upward on the side of the scoring contestant.

11–12. *Tsuzukete hajime* (resume fighting—begin). As he says "*tsuzukete*," standing in a forward stance, the referee extends his arms outward with his palms facing the contestants. As he says "*hajime*," he turns the palms of the hands and brings them rapidly toward one another, at the same time stepping back.

(Continued)

(Continued)

13. *Kiken* ("renunciation"—win by default). The referee points with his index finger toward the renouncing contestant's line, then announces a win to the opponent.

14–16. *Shikkaku* ("leave the area"—disqualification from the tournament). The referee points first upward at 45° in the direction of the offender, then motions out and behind with the announcement "*Aka shikkaku!*" or "*Ao shikkaku!*," depending on whether the competitor is wearing a red or blue belt. He then announces a win for the opponent.

17–18. *Hikiwake* (draw). When time is up and the scores are equal, or no scores have been awarded, the referee crosses his arms, then extends them with the palms showing to the front.

19. Category I offense. The referee crosses his open hands with the edge of one wrist on the edge, or the other at chest level.

20. Category II offense. The referee points with a bent arm at the face of the offender.

21. *Keikoku* (warning, to the feet). *Ippon* penalty. The referee indicates a category I or II offence, then points with his index finger downward at a 45° angle in the direction of the offender, and awards *ippon* (one point) to the opponent.

22. *Shugo* (judges called). The referee calls the judges at the end of the match or bout, or to recommend *shikkaku*.

23. *Hansoku chui* (warning, to the body). *Nihon* penalty. The referee indicates a category I or II offense, then points with his index finger horizontally in the direction of the offender and awards *nihon* (two points) to the opponent.

24. *Hansoku* (warning, to the face, disqualification). The referee indicates a category I or II offense, then points with his index finger upward at 45° in the direction of the offender, then awards a win to the opponent.

(Continued)

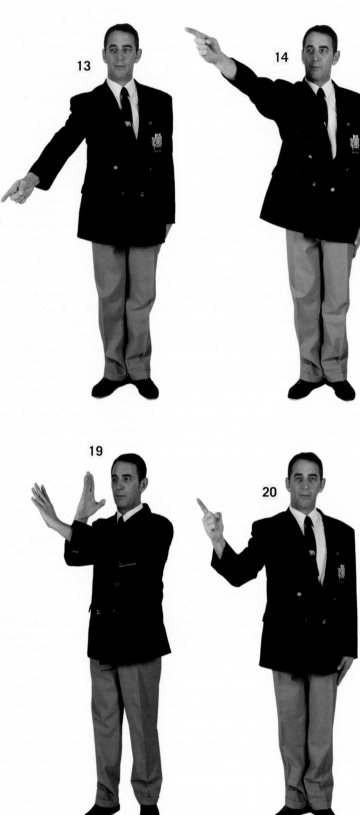

(Continued)

25. *Aiuchi* (simultaneous scoring techniques). No point is awarded to either contestant. The referee brings the fists together in front of the chest.

26. *Torimasen* (no score). A move is unacceptable as a scoring technique. The referee crosses his arms, then makes a cutting motion, palms downward. When the referee uses this signal to the judges, followed by the signal for reconsideration, it means that the technique was deficient in one or more of the six scoring criteria.

27. *Aka* or *ao* scored first. The referee indicates to the judges that *aka* scored first by bringing the open right hand to the palm of the left hand. If *ao* was first, the left hand points into the right hand.

28. Feigning or exaggerating injury. The referee holds both hands to the face to indicate to the judges a category II offense.

29. *Jogai* (exit from the match area). The referee indicates an exit to the judges by pointing with the index finger to the match area boundary on the side of the offender.

30. Avoiding combat. The referee makes a circling motion with the downturned index finger to indicate to the judges a category II offense.

31. Cancel last decision. When an award or penalty has been given in error, the referee turns toward the contestant, announces *aka* or *ao*, crosses his arms, then makes a cutting motion, palms downward, to indicate that the last decision has been cancelled.

32. *Mubobi* (self-endangerment). The referee touches his face then, turning the hand edge forward, moves it back and forth to indicate to the judges that the contestant has endangered himself.

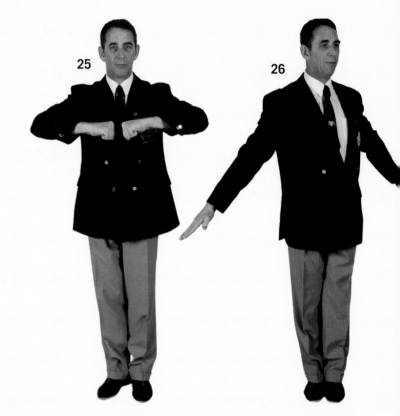

Competition *kata*

WKF competition rules

The area for *kata* competition is the same as that for the *kumite* competition. It must be flat and devoid of any hazard. The area is also covered with *tatami* (matting) and large enough to permit an uninterrupted performance.

Contestants are expected to perform a compulsory *kata* (*shitei*) and a free selection *kata* (*tokui*). These *kata* must be from one of the four major schools of karate-do: Goju, Shito, Shoto, or Wado systems.

No variation of *kata* is allowed in the *shitei* rounds. When performing in *tokui* rounds, the *kata* must be chosen from the list of *kata* that are recognized by the WKF *kata* list (shown on page 154). Variations of these *kata* will be accepted if taught by the organization to which the competitor belongs.

Contestants must perform a different *kata* in each round. Once they have performed with that *kata*, it cannot be used again. They can perform a *shitei kata* or a *tokui kata* in a *repechâge* (round).

In the finals of team *kata* competition, the two finalist teams will perform their chosen *kata* from the *tokui* list of *kata*. They will then perform a demonstration of the meaning of the *kata* (*bunkai*). The time allowed for the demonstration of *bunkai* is five minutes. The official timekeeper will start the countdown clock as the team members perform the bow. On completion of the *kata* performance, the timekeeper will stop the clock on the final bow after the *bunkai*. A team that exceeds the allowed five-minute period will be disqualified. The use of ancillary equipment, traditional weapons and additional apparel is not allowed.

Kata judges

There can either be three or five *kata* judges for each match, and none of them must hold the same nationality of the competitors if it is an international competition.

Operation of a *kata* match

At the start of each bout and in answer to their names, two contestants—one wearing a red belt (*aka*); the other a blue belt (*ao*)—will line up at the perimeter of the match area. They will both be facing the chief *kata* judge. Following a bow to the judging panel, *ao* will step back out of the match area. *Aka* will move to the starting position, call out the name of the *kata* to be performed and begin. When *aka* has completed the *kata* and left the area, *ao* will perform the *kata* while *aka* watches.

When *ao* finishes and leaves the area, both competitors will return to the match area perimeter and await the decision of the judging panel.

If the *kata* does not conform to the rules, or if there is an irregularity, the chief judge may call the other judges in order to reach a verdict. If a contestant is disqualified, the chief judge will cross and uncross the flags, as in the *kumite torimasen* signal.

After completion of both *kata*, the contestants will stand, side by side, on the perimeter. The chief judge will call for a decision (*hantei*) and blow a two-tone blast on the whistle, whereupon the judges will cast their vote.

Each judge's decision will be indicated by a raised red flag for *aka* or a raised blue flag for *ao*. No ties are permitted. The competitor who receives the majority vote will be declared the winner and the announcement made. The competitors will bow to each other, then to the judging panel, and leave the area.

Criteria for a decision

The *kata* must be performed with competence and must demonstrate a clear understanding of the traditional principles it contains, including:

- **A realistic demonstration of the *kata* meaning.**
- **Understanding of the techniques being used (*bunkai*).**
- **Good timing, rhythm, speed, balance, and focus of power (*kime*).**
- **Correct and proper use of breathing as an aid to *kime*.**
- **Correct focus of attention (*chakugan*) and concentration.**
- **Correct stances (*dachi*) with proper tension in the legs and feet flat on the floor.**
- **Proper tension in the abdomen (*hara*), and no bobbing up and down of the hips when moving.**
- **Correct *kihon* of the style being demonstrated.**
- **Evaluation of the performance, with a view to discerning other points such as the difficulty of the *kata* being presented.**
- **In team *kata*, synchronization without external cues is an added factor to take into consideration.**

Right: The opening move of the advanced Shotokan *kata* *unsu*. The stance is *neko-ashi dachi* (left cat stance) and both hands are held in *ippon nukite*.

Karate titles

The Dai Nippon Butokukai, the controlling body for martial arts, accepted karate into the organization in 1931. One of its stipulations was that karate had to have a grading system and test given for degrees.

The Dai Nippon Butokukai was established in 1895 by the Japanese government to oversee the martial arts. In 1902, the organization created two titles to be awarded to outstanding martial artists. These titles were *hanshi*, the highest award, and *kyoshi*, which was later changed to *tasshi*. These titles were initially awarded to martial artists who practiced judo or kendo. After karate was admitted, a third title was created, *renshi*, which was below *hanshi* and *kyoshi*. In 1935, three karate men received the title of *renshi*. They were Chojun Miyagi, founder of Goju-ryu; Ueshimi, founder of Kushin-ryu; and Yasuhiro Konishi, founder of Shindo-jinen-ryu, thus becoming the first karate men to receive a title in karate. In 1938, Yasuhiro Konishi was selected to be an examiner for candidates for the title of *renshi* and was on the board of examiners that awarded the title to Gichin Funakoshi. This was ironic, as Konishi was a student of Funakoshi.

At present, most karate organizations use either a five- or ten-*dan* grading system and a ten- or six-*kyu* grading system. Beginners start as white belts, working their way through the belt colors until they reach black belt. *Kyu* steps are often referred to as "boy" level, and *dan* steps as "man" level.

JAPANESE RANKING TERMS

Sho dan	1st degree	Black belt
Ni dan	2nd degree	Black belt
San dan	3rd degree	Black belt
Yon dan	4th degree	Black belt
Go dan	5th degree	Black belt
Roku dan	6th degree	Black belt
Shichi dan	7th degree	Black belt
Hachi dan	8th degree	Black belt
Ku dan	9th degree	Black belt
Jyu dan	10th degree	Black belt
Jik kyu	10th kyu	
Kyo kyu	9th kyu	
Hachi kyu	8th kyu	
Shichi kyu	7th kyu	
Rok kyu	6th kyu	
Go kyu	5th kyu	
Yon kyu	4th kyu	
San kyu	3rd kyu	
Ni kyu	2nd kyu	
Ik kyu	1st kyu	

BELT COLORS

Yellow belt	*Kiiro obi*
Orange belt	*Orenji obi*
Purple belt	*Murasaki obi*
Blue belt	*Ao obi*
Green belt	*Midori obi*
Brown belt	*Cha obi*
Black belt	*Kuro obi*

Left: Three members of a *kata* team practicing for a competition.

Appendixes

- Correct tying of the *obi*

- Glossary of terms

- Glossary of Japanese terminology

- WKF major *kata* allowed in competition

- Fighting flag signals

Left and below: Learning how to tie your *obi* (belt) correctly is an important skill that all *karate-ka* must learn.

Correct tying of the *obi* (belt)

It is quite interesting to see all the variations of belts that can be tied around a *karate-ka*'s waist. Here I have shown the method of tying an *obi* that I was taught while training in Japan.

1. Place the *obi* in front of you, holding it in both hands.
2. Ensure the *obi* is longer on the right side.
3. Prepare to pull the *obi* across the waist.
4. Pull the *obi* in tightly across the waist.
5. Pull the right side of the *obi* around and across the back (side view).
6. Continue pulling the *obi* all the way around the body.

7. Hold the *obi* firmly in the left hand, as the long end is pulled through with the right hand.

8. Continue to pull the *obi* all the way through with the right hand.

9. Start to wrap the *obi* around the body again with the right hand.

10. As before, continue to pull the *obi* across the back with the right hand.

11. Encircle the back again with the *obi*.

12. Bring the *obi* through, having wrapped it around the back twice.

13. Pull the end of the *obi* all the way across the body with the right hand.

14. Cross the *obi* in front of the body, ensuring the *obi* end in the right hand rests on top of the other belt layers.

15. With the left hand, pull both the layers of *obi* wrapped around the body, creating a gap.

(Continued)

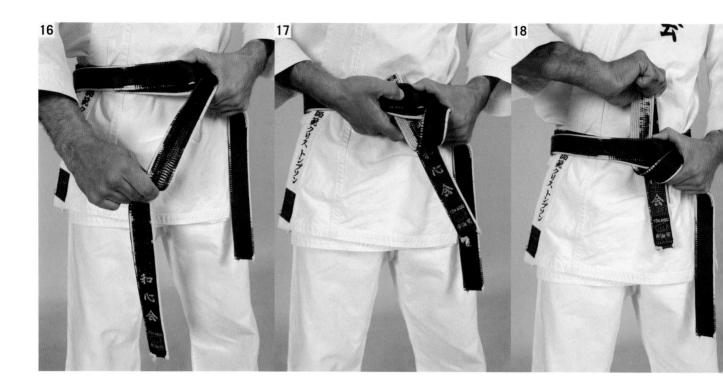

(Continued)

16. Prepare to pull the end of the *obi* in the right hand underneath both layers of the *obi*.

17. Pull the *obi* up, underneath the two layers, with the right hand.

18. Continue to pull the right end of the *obi* through.

19. Ensure that the *obi* is pulled up tightly as it comes through to the end.

20. Bring down the *obi* length that has come up, underneath the other layers.

21. As the *obi* is brought down with the right hand, begin to

bring the other end of the *obi* up with the left hand.

22. Drop the *obi* in the right hand across the other length of *obi*.

23. Bring the *obi* in the right hand up, underneath the end of the *obi*.

24. Continue pulling both ends together to form a knot.

25. Pull the *obi* together as firmly as possible.

26. Pull the knot firmly, and adjust the position of the knot ready to drop the end down in the right hand.

27. A correctly tied *obi*.

Glossary of terms

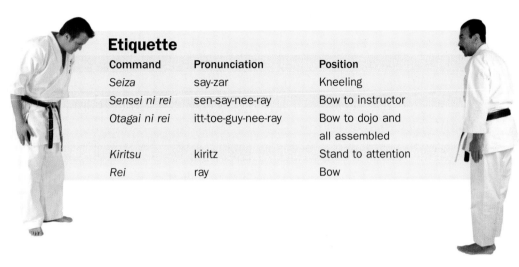

Etiquette

Command	Pronunciation	Position
Seiza	say-zar	Kneeling
Sensei ni rei	sen-say-nee-ray	Bow to instructor
Otagai ni rei	itt-toe-guy-nee-ray	Bow to dojo and all assembled
Kiritsu	kiritz	Stand to attention
Rei	ray	Bow

Karate technique

	Te	Kind of hand
1	*Seiken*	Fore fist
2	*Uraken*	Back fist
3	*Tettsui*	Bottom fist
4	*Ippon ken*	One-knuckle fist
5	*Nakadaka ippon ken*	Middle finger one knuckle
6	*Haito*	Ridge hand
7	*Shuto*	Knife hand
8	*Nihon nukite*	Two-finger spear hand
9	*Ippon nukite*	One-finger spear hand
10	*Yonhon nukite*	Spear hand
11	*Teisho*	Palm heel
12	*Koko*	Tiger mouth hand
13	*Ude*	Forearm
14	*Empi/hiji*	Elbow

	Ashi	Kind of foot
1	*Hiza*	Knee
2	*Sokuto*	Foot edge
3	*Kakato*	Heel
4	*Koshi*	Ball of foot
5	*Haisoku*	Instep
6	*Ashi-barai*	Foot sweep
7	*Surikomi*	One step

	Shishei	Form
1	*Musubi dachi*	Informal attention stance
2	*Heisoku dachi*	Formal attention stance
3	*Shiko dachi*	Open leg stance
4	*Kiba dachi*	Straddle leg stance
5	*Neko ashi dachi*	Cat stance
6	*Hachiji dachi*	Ready stance (as in *yoi*)
7	*Zenkutsu dachi*	Long stance
8	*Sagi ashi dachi*	Crane stance
9	*Kokutsu dachi*	Back stance
10	*Sanchin dachi*	Hourglass stance
11	*Shizentai dachi*	Natural stance

	Uke	Blocking
1	*Jodan uke*	Forearm block
2	*Shuto uke*	Knife-hand block
3	*Gedan barai*	Downward block
4	*Morote uke*	Augmented forearm block
5	*Uchi uke (gaiwan)*	Inner block (little finger side)
6	*Soto uke (naiwan)*	Outer block (thumb side)
7	*Uraken uke*	Backfist block
8	*Haisho uke*	Backhand block

	Tsuki waza	Punching
1	*Jun zuki*	Lunge punch
2	*Gyaku zuki*	Reverse punch
3	*Yama zuki*	Double fist punch
4	*Furi zuki*	Swing punch
5	*Shita zuki*	Lower punch

Left: *Tobi-yoko-geri* (jumping side kick), a technique originally devised to knock an opponent from a horse.

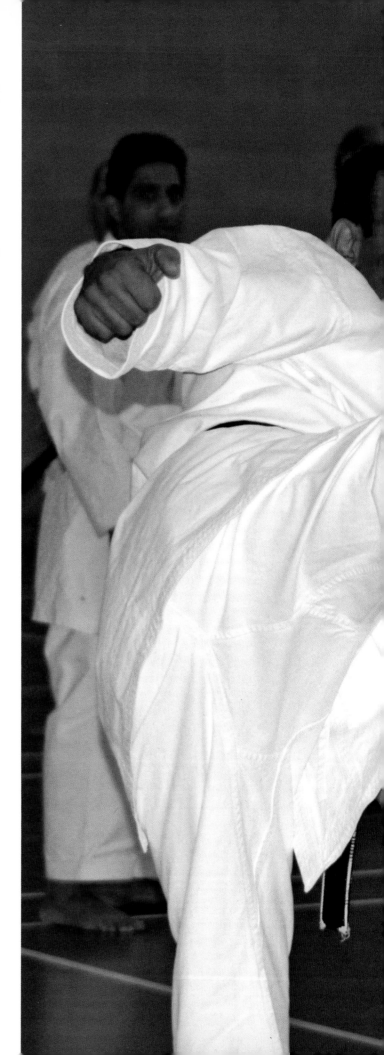

	Uchi waza	**Striking**
1	*Kakuto uchi*	Wrist strike
2	*Tettsui uchi*	Bottom fist strike
3	*Shuto uchi*	Knife hand strike
4	*Haito uchi*	Ridge hand strike
5	*Teisho uchi*	Palm heel strike
6	*Empi uchi*	Elbow strike
7	*Uraken uchi*	Back fist strike

	Keri waza	**Kicking**
1	*Mae-geri*	Front kick
2	*Mae-geri-keage*	Front snap kick
3	*Mawashi-geri*	Roundhouse kick
4	*Nidan-geri*	Double kick
5	*Hiza-geri*	Knee kick
6	*Yoko-geri*	Side kick
7	*Yoko-geri-keage*	Side snap kick
8	*Mikazuki-geri*	Crescent kick
9	*Mukozune-geri*	Shin kick
10	*Fumikomi-geri*	Stamping kick
11	*Sokuto-fumikomi*	Foot edge stamping kick
12	*Ushiro-geri*	Back kick
13	*Ura-mawashi-geri*	Hooking roundhouse kick
14	*Ushiro-mawashi-geri*	Back spinning kick
15	*Tobi-yoko-geri*	Jumping side kick
16	*Tobi-mawashi-geri*	Jumping roundhouse kick
17	*Tobi-nidan-geri*	Jumping double kick
18	*Tobi-ushiro-geri*	Jumping back kick
19	*Kansetsu-geri*	Joint kick

JAPANESE NUMBERS ONE TO TEN

ichi	one
ni	two
san	three
shi	four
go	five
roku	six
shichi	seven
hachi	eight
ku	nine
ju	ten

Right: Students practicing kicks.

Glossary of Japanese terminology

aiuchi	Simultaneous scoring techniques
aka	Red belt
ao	Blue belt
bo	Six-foot staff
Budo	Precepts of the *samurai*
bunkai	Application of the *kata* moves
chakugan	Verbal warning
chuan fa	Chinese fighting system
Dai Nippon Butokukai	Governing body for Japanese martial arts
dan	Black-belt level
deshi	Student
do-gi	Karate suit (correct Japanese terminology)
dojo kun	Club/style maxim
gaijin	Derogatory name for foreigners
gasshuku	Extended training camp
gi	Karate suit (common use)
Giko Funakoshi	Third son of Gichin Funakoshi
Gogen Yamaguchi	A student of Chojun Miyagi who became the senior instructor in Japan of the Goju style
Goju-ryu	Style of karate founded by Chojun Miyagi
Hanko-ryu	The name Mabuni gave his style before changing it to Shito-ryu
hanshi	Japanese senior rank for a *karate-ka*
hansoku	Disqualification
hansoku chui	Warning with two points going to opponent
hantai	Decision
hara	Abdomen
hente waza	Using the same limb to both block and strike
hikiwake	Draw
honbu	Headquarters
ikken hisatsu	To kill with one strike

ippon	One-point score
irimi	Entering
ji yu kumite	Freestyle sparring
jissen	Actual fighting
jogai	Outside the competing area
ju jitsu	The original martial art from which judo is derived
junbi undo	Warming up exercises
kakushi waza	Secret techniques in *kata*
kama	Sickle
Kannryo Higoanna	Teacher of Chojun Miyagi and Kenwa Mabuni (sometimes the name is pronounced Higashionna)
kansetsu waza	Techniques aimed at the joints in the body
karate jutsu	Karate fighting
karate ni sentenashi	A Japanese concept
karate-do	The way of karate
karate-ka	One who practices karate
kata	Form; prearranged set of attack and defense movements
kawashi	Evasion
keikoku	Warning with one point to opponent
keri	Kick
kiai	Releasing the energy in the body through a huge shout
kihon	Basic fundamental techniques of karate
kiken	Win by default
kime	Focused power
kokyu	Correct breathing
kumite	Fighting
kung fu	Chinese martial arts
Kyokushinkai	Japanese style of karate created by Matsutatsu Oyama
kyoshi/tasshi	Japanese senior rank for a *karate-ka*, but lower than *hanshi*
kyu	Color-belt level
makiwara	Striking board

meisei juku	Boarding house for Okinawan students
menkyo	Teaching diploma
Motobu Choki	Famed karate fighter
mubobi	Fighter is causing self-endangerment
nagashi	Flowing
nage waza	Throwing techniques
Naha	Okinawan town
nihon	Two-point score
no kachi	Winner of competition
nogare	Escaping
nunchuku	Rice flails
obi	Belt
ohyo gumite	Prearranged pairwork
Okinawan *te*	Okinawan fighting system
osaekomi waza	Immobilization techniques
otagai ni rei	Bow to everybody
rei	To bow
reishiki	Dojo discipline
renshi	Japanese senior rank for a *karate-ka*, but lower than *kyoshi*
ryu	School of karate
sai	Metal-pronged fork
samurai	Japanese warrior
sanbon	Three-point score
Satsuma clan	Japanese warrior group
sempai	A *karate-ka* who is senior in rank
sensei	Teacher
sensei ni rei	Bow to instructor
shiai	Competition match
shihan	Master
shikkaku	Disqualification from tournament
shime waza	Choking techniques
shin gi tai	Unite your mind, body, and spirit
Shindo Yoshin-ryu ju jitsu	A style of ju jitsu
shingi	Mind and body not working together
shitei	Compulsory *kata*
Shito-ryu	Style of karate founded by Kenwa Mabuni
shobu hajime	Start the match
shobu ippon	A fighting system of a tournament
shomen ni rei	Bow to the front
Shorin-ryu	Name given to Shaolin style
Shotokan	Style of karate founded by Gichin Funakoshi
shugo	Judges called
shuhari	A Japanese concept
Shuri	Okinawan town
sun dome	To control a technique to within one inch of target
taisabaki	Hip shifting
tameshigeri	Test by cutting
tameshiwari	Test by breaking
tatami	Matted flooring
te	Abbreviated name for Okinawan fighting
tekko	Metal knuckle-dusters
tode	Okinawan fighting system
tokui	Free-choice *kata*
Tomari	Okinawan town
tonfa	Rice-grinding flails
torimasen	No score
tsuki	Punch
tsuzukete hajime	Begin fighting again
uchi	Strike
Wado-ryu	Style of karate founded by Hirinori Ohtsuka
waza	Technique
wazari	Half-point score
wushu	Chinese fighting system
yakusoku gumite	Prearranged pairwork
yame	Stop
zanshin	Awareness

WKF major *kata* allowed in competition

GOJU-RYU

kururunfa
saifa
sanchin
sanseru
seipai
seisan
seiyunchin
shisochin
suparimpei
tensho

WADO-RYU

wanshu
naihanchi
kushanku
passai
rohai
niseishi
seishan
chinto
jion
jitte

SHOTOKAN

bassai-dai
jiin
bassai-sho
gankaku
enpi
jion
hangetsu
wankan
jitte
unsu
kanku-dai
meikyo
kanku-sho
sochin
tekki-nidan
nijushiho sho
tekki-sandan
goju shiho-sho
tekki-shodan
chinte
goju shiho-dai

SHITO-RYU

annanko
papuren
chatanyara kushanku
bassai dai
sochin
nipaipo
bassai sho
niseishi
sanchin
heiku
kururunfa
paiku
jiin
kosokun shiho
naifanchin nidan
jion
kosokun sho
naifanchin shodan
jitte
kosokun dai
seisan
matsukaze
chinto
naifanchin sandan
matsumura basai
unshu
seipai
pachu
sanseiru
hamucho
rohai
seienchin
jyuroku
saifa
shisochin
annan
suparimpei
tomari bassai
gojushiho
tensho
wanshu
chinte
aoyagi (seiryu)

Fighting flag signals

IPPON

NIHON

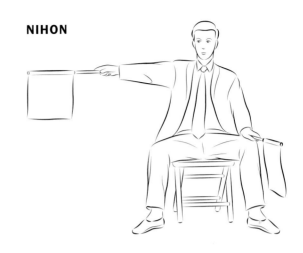

SANBON

FOUL

CATEGORY I OFFENSE

(Continued)

(Continued)

CATEGORY II OFFENSE (A)

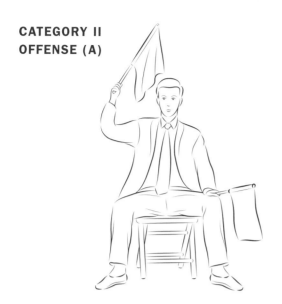

CATEGORY II OFFENSE (B)

JOGAI

KEIKOKU

HANSOKU CHUI

HANSOKU

TORIMASEN (A)

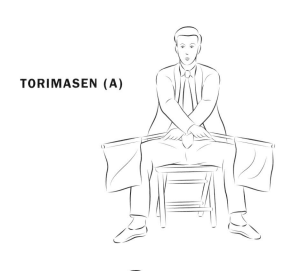

TORIMASEN (B)

AIUCHI

MIENAI

Index

Credits and acknowledgements

All photography is by Mike Holdsworth, with the exception of those photographs supplied by Chris Thompson on the following pages: 2, 12–13, 22, 23, 35 (top), 36, 40, 62 (bottom), 66 (bottom), 67, 94, 95, 112, 113, 124, 126, 138, 149, 157. Chris Thompson also supplied the Japanese character for "karate" used on pages 3, 7, 11, 37, 125, and 141.

New Holland Publishers would like to thank the following:

Yoshinobu Ohta, Chief Instructor for JKA (Japanese Karate Association), England for demonstrating *kata*; Neville Smith, Alison Thompson, Sarah Vallé, Jason Brown, Alex Thick, and James Thompson for their modeling and assistance; Ed Semple of Sleeping Storm Dojo, Epsom for the use of his facilities; and Penny Brown for the index.